DATE DUE

CONVERSATIONS
with
CONDUCTORS

CONVERSATIONS
with
CONDUCTORS

Bruno Walter, Sir Adrian Boult, Leonard Bernstein,
Ernest Ansermet, Otto Klemperer, Leopold Stokowski

Edited by
ROBERT CHESTERMAN

Photographs by Godfrey MacDomnic
(Photograph of Bruno Walter by Fred Plaut)

ROWMAN AND LITTLEFIELD
Totowa, New Jersey

167975

First published in Great Britain in 1976 by Robson Books,
London.

Printed in Great Britain.

For Marguerite

Contents

Introduction

The principal conversations in this book are taken from recordings made between the years 1966 and 1969, a period when, as a radio producer for the Canadian Broadcasting Corporation, I was fortunate to talk at length in front of a microphone with a number of distinguished conductors. The interviews with Bruno Walter and Leopold Stokowski fall outside this series.

In the early sixties I started to prepare a retrospective study for radio of Bruno Walter as man and artist, undertaken in collaboration with Columbia Masterworks in New York, the company for which he made his last recordings and which represented his final legacy. In the closing years of his life Walter lived in California, where the hot, dry climate suited him best. The orchestral sessions took place in Los Angeles with a pick-up orchestra, the members of which were mostly émigrés from central Europe, like himself. By this time, the concert appearances of the octogenarian conductor were few, but, as it turned out, Vancouver benefited from a certain proximity to his Beverly Hills home, for Walter agreed to make the thousand-mile journey up the West Coast to direct the Vancouver Symphony Orchestra on one or two memorable occasions. I was able to attend performances which both fascinated and intrigued me: how could an average provincial orchestra play like this? Part of the answer was provided by a CBC television film made on one of Walter's visits. Directed by Gene Lawrence, it included rehearsal sessions and a short chat—recorded in Beverly Hills—between Walter and Albert Goldberg, a Californian music critic. Goldberg asked the question: 'How does a conductor obtain the results he wants?' The brief conversation which followed later formed part of the radio broadcast devoted to Walter, his words providing much of the inspiration to record at greater length with other famous conductors, most of whom were also in the twilight of their years and of similar vast experience.

The television film itself was, for the period, a good one. But these were early days and even by the mid-sixties I found most radio and television interviews on musical topics frustratingly brief and superficial. This feeling of dissatisfaction extended to John Freeman's famous BBC television 'Face to Face' interview with Otto Klemperer. Much as I admired the technique, I felt a sense of missed opportunity. Although there were memorable moments, I remember wishing that Freeman had explored the musical aspects in greater depth; in the event, the half-hour—entertaining as it was—lacked many of the insights which I had expected.

Partly at the instigation of my programme director and good friend, Peter Garvie, and with much support from John Roberts, then the head of music for CBC Radio in Toronto, I decided to embark upon a series of conversations which we hoped would avoid the pitfalls of formats dictated by the requirements of time.

It was decided to begin by approaching Sir Adrian Boult early in 1966. I wrote and asked if he would be willing to devote several consecutive days to sitting in front of a microphone answering some questions. The subject was to be the art of the conductor. I suggested an hour or so for each session. To my delight and astonishment Sir Adrian replied virtually by return of post, suggesting a period in July when he would be free.

I travelled to London and Sir Adrian asked me to join him for lunch at his club, the Athenaeum. When I arrived he was waiting for me—as indeed I discovered in subsequent days he would be, sitting in the designated studio at Broadcasting House at least twenty minutes before our appointment, quietly reading a book.

I suppose in my state of considerable nervousness I wanted to impress with my knowledge. I had researched long and arduously for these sessions. I observed that, of course, it was Elgar who had proposed him for membership at this hallowed institution. Sir Adrian was astonished and asked me how I had discovered that one; he had forgotten. From that moment I began to enjoy myself greatly and benefit from his extraordinary kindness and consideration. Godfrey MacDomnic's photos capture to perfection the essence of this grand English gentleman, whose tolerance for many quite naïve points I was to put to him later was generosity itself.

The following year Leonard Bernstein said he would record for us. His fiftieth birthday was approaching and, through his secretary, he agreed it might be a suitable occasion to talk about himself and his feelings on music in general. It was indicated that only one session would be possible and an afternoon was set aside in a CBS studio in downtown New York.

I had spent two hours the previous day at Bernstein's Park Avenue apartment, where he had invited me to explain what I had in mind. As I rose in a private elevator to his penthouse, I little expected the greeting that awaited me: it amounted to an appalled acceptance of the valuable time he had consented to give up, coupled with the realization that a fiftieth birthday was the last thing he wished to contemplate. My discomfort increased further as he learned of my intention to include critical assessment of his musicianship in the main body of the birthday tribute. I recall that for much of this meeting he was stretched out on the couch in his working den, but this small item of information raised him from the reclining posture. The discussion which followed about his critics was repeated the next afternoon in a more reflective manner and in front of a microphone. It was settled that I was to talk with him about conducting and his career in general and that Richard Franko Goldman, the American musicologist, was to touch upon composing and American music, areas which I did not feel equipped to handle.

Bernstein arrived in the studio, coat over his shoulders, and once seated in front of the microphone became very expansive. His opening response to my first tentative question took some twenty minutes. His co-operation was complete and I felt indebted by the end of the afternoon.

Arriving in Geneva in September of the following year, 1968, I was to meet a completely different and, again, totally original personality. This was Ernest Ansermet, then in his eighties and living in an atmosphere in complete contrast to New York and the unnecessary stresses and strains which that vast city imposes. I had long felt that Ansermet had not received the attention he deserved. His associations in the early decades of the century—with Stravinsky, Debussy, Picasso, Satie and Diaghilev, among countless others—encompassing as they did the worlds of ballet, opera and theatre, represented an extraordinary link with the creative forces which abounded in Paris in those years. But when I first went to his home, one in a row of terraced houses on the Rue Bellôt, Ansermet told me he had resisted all blandishments from his publisher to write his autobiography. 'Perhaps later,' he said. He

went on, 'I was charmed when I received your letter, from so far away.'
It was apparent that my good fortune in being able to sit with him in a
Swiss Radio studio for three consecutive days rested on my being
outside the European circle of music critics and writers.

Each afternoon I would be driven through the narrow streets of the
Old Town to collect him. Ansermet always came to the door himself;
with the white beard he was still very imposing, although a little bent
with age. The cab drivers would always address him as *maître* and
everyone knew him on sight.

After three lengthy sessions, often rapping on the table in front of
him with great energy and frequently chuckling infectiously with his
deep gurgling laugh, he told me, 'You must come again, we could talk
for hours.' But sadly this was not to be: early in the new year, three
months after recording the complete *Firebird* with the New Philharmonia Orchestra, which followed the taping of these conversations,
Ansermet died.

Peter Heyworth, music critic of the London *Observer*, who had
already recorded a number of talks for me, heard the Ansermet broadcasts which the BBC repeated after their first hearing in Canada. At
my suggestion, he agreed to approach Otto Klemperer with the proposal
that we should make a recording on similar lines. Our correspondence
with Klemperer was conducted through his daughter, Lotte, and to our
delight he too agreed to talk in front of a microphone, provided we
would visit him at his home in Zurich. These conversations, which
took place in September 1969, have already been published in a much
more extended form, incorporating material from other sources,[1] but
both Lotte Klemperer and Peter Heyworth kindly agreed that I could
incorporate a section of the CBC conversation in this book. Although I
did not put questions to Klemperer myself, I wished this inclusion
because of certain cross-references that occur in relation to the other
contributors. The different viewpoints on Toscanini, who was clearly
such an influential figure, are a case in point.

Klemperer was the most awe-inspiring person I have ever met.
Although I knew he was very large of stature, I recall how enormous he
seemed at that first meeting in his Zurich apartment. His daughter, with
great good humour, made things most comfortable for us. During the

---

[1]*Conversations with Klemperer*, compiled and edited by Peter Heyworth, published in 1973 by
Victor Gollancz Ltd., London.

recording sessions we had to use the bedroom next door to set up our recording equipment, and as the talk from the next room went on the tape I would stare at the colossal brass bedstead in front of me, underneath which was a pair of the largest slippers imaginable. At each side of the bed was a picture, one of the young Goethe and the other of Napoleon. Klemperer would always be seated in a chair by the window when we arrived, usually reading a book or perusing a score and with numerous pipes on the table beside him. On one occasion he had the radio on; it was a broadcast of Handel's *Messiah* and his recording of the work. I asked him if he was pleased with what he heard. 'It is good,' he said.

In total contrast to Klemperer's powerful and forbidding presence was his wonderful sense of humour. I think the biggest surprise was an evening spent after recording, when we all listened to a gramophone record of Tom Lehrer made at the 'hungry i', a night club in San Francisco. The irreverence of the two items he wanted us to hear from the disc, one parodying Alma Mahler Werfel and the other a satire on the Pope, amused him hugely. Throughout he thumped his stick on the floor in time to Lehrer's lyrics, roaring his sideways laugh.

The contribution from Leopold Stokowski breaks away from the conversational form, his words forming the basis of an imaginative, if controversial, sound documentary compiled by Glenn Gould, to whom I am indebted, with Stokowski, for allowing me to include an extract in this book. It was recorded in New York as part of a combined project of the CBC and National Educational Television. Gould felt that an explanation was needed for 'the rather off-beat ambience' of the material. He wrote to me: 'Stokowski never quite got used to the idea, when recording, that my audio needs were utterly different from those of a television programme. Since the NET crew insisted on blowing the fuses in his apartment once every half-hour on average, and since Stokowski clearly became fatigued towards the end of both sessions, I wound up with a grand total of some fifty minutes of usable material. When I began to realize that I would not have the opportunity to question him about matters musical, I deliberately set out for a mood-piece and gauged my questions accordingly. Certainly, in terms of the rather impressionistic result I was after for radio, I was more than happy with Stokowski's responses.'

In order to achieve the particular effect he wanted for the programme, Glenn Gould used a stereophonic musical montage behind Stokowski's

words and his own questions were edited out. Without the advantage
of sound, it is obviously impossible to reproduce the total effect for the
reader, but I hope this explanation may illuminate the printed mono-
logue.

I have to register also two disappointments in the compilation of this
volume. In the early summer of 1971 I recorded with Eugene Ormandy
in Ames, Iowa, a small university town in the heart of the American
Corn Belt, during a tour of the Philadelphia Orchestra. A successful
broadcast was unfortunately followed by Ormandy's denial of permission to publish. The reasons for his decision remain incomprehensible,
particularly since he shed considerable light on his early beginnings
and, notably, on his appointment to the musical directorship of the
Philadelphia Orchestra in 1938, following in the footsteps of the
renowned Leopold Stokowski.

Early in 1974, in bleak January weather, I travelled to Berlin and
undertook a similar series of sessions with Herbert von Karajan.
Regrettably, Karajan also was unable to grant permission to print, but
this for reasons of copyright.

In conclusion, I should mention that I have had to edit all the conversations which appear in this book in order to achieve a certain
conciseness. In some cases I have clarified various phrases, since, at
times, the spoken word has an emphasis which does not convey quite
the same intent in written form. These instances are few, however, and
I have taken great care to retain the essence of the original utterance
without changing the meaning. Too often with a radio programme the
permanent taped record comes to reside on a dusty archive shelf and
after one or two broadcasts it is forgotten. With this modest publication
I hope that the thoughts and viewpoints of these famous musicians will
be more to the fore when any future substantial study of the twentieth-
century conductor comes to be written.

By way of a postscript, I recall one memorable experience which also
played a part in the inspiration for these conversations. Incredible as
it seemed to me at the time, my first assignment as a fledgling music
producer was an extraordinary morning spent with Sir Thomas
Beecham. This was early in 1960 when Beecham, making what was to
be his final tour of guest appearances in North America, arrived at the
Hotel Vancouver fresh from Seattle, after a stormy set-to with a

member of the local press corps. Terrified at the thought of putting any questions to this illustrious figure, I asked a local music critic, Ian Docherty, to undertake what I sensed might be an arduous assignment. It was nothing of the sort. As a prelude to a vastly entertaining hour, we were greeted at eleven o'clock on a Friday morning by a Sir Thomas clad in opulent, dark blue robe, a freshly-lit cigar to hand, and an enquiry if we would all like gins with which to open the proceedings. 'Did you say your name was Chesterman? A relation of the double bass player in my orchestra?' he asked. I had to say I was not. 'Pity,' he said, 'A professor of the double bass.' It was later I learnt that at such times Sir Thomas was at his most benign and expansive.

Nevertheless, there was an echo of the previous day's eruption when, in closing, the interviewer suggested that he had not, perhaps, gone beyond a certain repertoire. This magnificent *faux pas* produced a characteristic coda from Sir Thomas: 'I've played five hundred and ninety pieces, if that's what you mean! That's just like a certain part of the press which goes on saying "Sir Thomas Beecham's favourite piece is so-and-so." It's not so! I play certain pieces—Mozart, Schubert, Haydn—because I am asked to do so. Everywhere. And the moment I put something else in, they say, "Oh, do play us something of Handel. Do play us something of Tchaikovsky. Do play us something of Wagner, or Beethoven." In Germany they want me to play Wagner and Beethoven, or Bruckner. In France they want me to play Debussy and Ravel. And so I do. In England they want me to play everything; it's the only country where I can play everything. What can you do? It's not for me to say to these people, you shan't have it. When I am going to appear in a place, I send about fifty pieces. I say choose for yourselves. They always pick the same things. It is just like the press that keeps on saying I'm bad-tempered and testy. I've never been testy in my life. I've given countless interviews and if you can find one single person to suggest that I've got a bad temper or I'm testy—peppery is the favourite, I, peppery!—find a single player in Europe, in the States, or anywhere, to whom I've ever been rude or impatient or even critical, beyond the usual scope of polite criticism which I am obliged to use . . . all right, publish his name! Let me hear it. And I've been going now for well over sixty years as a conductor. The only time I'm ever testy is when some pertinacious, uncontrollable member of the press insists on invading my privacy, ringing me at two-thirty in the morning, waiting in the lobby downstairs, rushing up to me saying,

"I must have an interview." I say, quite quietly, "I can't do it now, I'm afraid. I'm on my way to rehearsal. I have to think about the music." Then he feels very affronted and says I'm testy. It is a delusion, Sir, it is an entire delusion. It is one of those legends and lies. The world is full of legends and lies about everybody, everybody. And they go on being perpetuated through the ages. This is what led the late Mr Ford, of immortal memory, to declare that all history is bunkum. I can tell you it is. I've read as much history as any man living, probably, apart from the two or three historical experts. And nearly all that I've read is manifestly incorrect. Because I've known everyone of any conse-quence for over fifty years in all countries. And all I read about these people is entirely incorrect, and a legend; in fact, bunkum. So there you are.'

Vancouver, 1976   R.C.

Bruno Walter

ALBERT GOLDBERG: *Dr Walter, you have a lovely place here in Beverly Hills. How long have you lived here?*

BRUNO WALTER: I came to California for the first time in 1927. I had to conduct a concert in the Hollywood Bowl and I fell in love with it at first sight. After that, I wished always to make my domicile here, but only in 1945 could I do so. Now, it is thirteen years that I live here and I have not yet regretted it. After many years in New York, with its *allegro furioso*, it was really a necessity for me to have this change. Now I am enjoying the *allegretto grazioso* of Beverly Hills, and it gives me the possibility of making a new contact with myself, of thinking, of meditating and—what's much more important for me—to learn. After sixty-four years of conducting, it was time to make a break.

Sixty-four years is a long time, Maestro. When and where did you start conducting?

I started conducting in 1894. So, sixty-four years ago. I started with my first opera in the opera house in Cologne, and in the fall of the same year I went to Hamburg, where the opera house had one great leader. That was Gustav Mahler. And in 1900 the Berlin Royal Opera engaged me as a conductor. There we were, three conductors whose names will not be quite unknown to you: one was Richard Strauss, one was Karl Muck, and the third one this humble and very youthful self.

In view of your long experience in conducting, maybe you'd like to say something about the art of conducting.

This is a very complex question. I must distinguish between the purely musical gifts of a conductor, his general human spiritual qualities, and even his moral standards. To speak about the first. There are two careers open for the conductor, and some of us have done both:

the operatic conductor and the symphony conductor. Now, you can imagine what a lonely operatic conductor has to strive for. There is the wide, wide field of operas and he must be at home in all this literature. There is the not less wide field of the symphonic literature and he must be at home in this just the same. Finally, he must have the personal qualities to live up to these very complicated and very strenuous demands on his talent and on his character.

There is one point I want to make which very rarely is considered by people who otherwise are at home in the world of music. This is the difference between the time of studying for the conductor and for the instrumentalist—the violin player or the cellist or the pianist. These three instrumentalists have their whole boyhood and their whole adolescence to study on their instrument, to perfect themselves in a technique. But the poor conductor, he cannot do the same. His instrument is this dragon with eighty or one hundred heads, and how should he practise on this instrument which is at his disposal for the first time when he begins his career? So he comes out as a naïve beginner, and this is a disadvantage which he can make up for only in years of practice. Because I tell you, from my own experience, he comes out for his first orchestra rehearsal and he has a very clear idea in his head how it should sound. But it is absolutely not what he expected. He is surrounded by musicians and there is a great confusion of sound before his ears and he doesn't know where to begin with his corrections and his admonitions to his musicians. This is one of the very great draw-backs in his activity. It takes a long time before he gets over it.

How does a conductor obtain the results he wants from his musicians?

This is the question for all of us. You know, one of the main questions is how to handle people, how to handle men, how to influence musicians by word, or by gesture, or by looks, and here his human qualities have very much to say in this question. If he is a man of warm heart and of sincerity, the musicians—even those who are far superior with regard to routine—will listen to him and will accept what he says. Then, the moral qualities of this man are very much decisive. But you see how manifold are the demands made on him and how versatile he has to be in order to fulfil these demands.

So the musical requirements are only part of the picture?

Only a very small part, permit me to say. If he is not a man who loves nature, if he does not know and love the meadow and the brook, he never could conduct Beethoven's *Pastoral* Symphony. And if he has not a passion, if he is not capable of ecstasy, he never could conduct *Tristan und Isolde* of Wagner; or, for instance, if he has not a romantic strain in his spiritual make-up, then he could not conduct the *Rhenish* Symphony of Schumann. So you see what the personality, the spiritual qualities of the conductor, really mean for his career and for the quality of his achievements.

Maestro, you've conducted all kinds of music, new and old, in your career. Now, when you look back, which composers mean the most to you? Which music do you find to be the most durable?

Let me go back to my childhood. The first star in my firmament was Beethoven, and I think this is quite understandable, because the youthful mind has a leaning to the powerful, to the Titanic, the Promethean. For years he was the ideal of my young musician's heart, and, at the same time, Schubert—which is a great contrast, of course. But Schubert seemed to me, and seems to me still today, music itself. So it was an elementary inclination of my heart which just loved him, loved him and loved his thematic substance. And after this came *the* great event: Wagner, and his *Tristan*. I heard it—I think I was a boy of thirteen or so—and he took possession of my soul and changed my life. That is not exaggerated, what I say. Well, and then it took some years, and then came Mozart into my life.

Mozart came late?

Mozart came late, later than the others, because you have to have maturity to understand beauty. Goethe said once that the tragic did not play too great a part in his life, but beauty always moved him to tears. And then you can very well imagine what it meant to me to meet Gustav Mahler when I came to Hamburg. He made me acquainted, playing for me his symphonies—at this time, when I came to Hamburg, in 1894, there were two symphonies there, the First and the Second— and I must say these are experiences in my life which still to this very day are overwhelming for me. Only a very short time ago I recorded the Second Symphony of Mahler. Last year I performed it in New York and then I fell ill; I could not finish the record. So, I finished it now and it came out very well. And when I heard the record I felt again this overwhelming power of Mahler's music, his personality, the spirituality of his being.

What about Bruckner?

Oh, Bruckner! This is a very special event in my life. I always preferred Bruckner, but I always had the feeling of being strange to his form, strange to the extremes of his expression. And one day, one fine day, I fell ill. I got pneumonia and I was laid up for weeks. And, you know, if you have a very serious kind of illness, then you make very great progress. It is a good recipe for human development. After I could leave the bed and regained my health, I had Bruckner. I had won the maturity now to understand him and his solemnity and his religious greatness, his nearness to all that is lofty and sublime. I had won an understanding and have not yet lost it so far.

Dr Walter, you used to conduct lots of contemporary music when you were younger. What is your relation now to contemporary music?

Let me say it is a friendly one. I do my best to understand it, and whenever I feel talent, sincerity and a musical inspiration, I am only very happy to acknowledge it and to perform it also. There are only two exceptions to which I must confess. I am very hostile to everything that is artificial, and this is, in my mind, atonality and the twelve-tone system. Let me just say this about atonality: if you want to speak correctly, then you must speak in a grammatical way; you must use your words as the laws of grammar tell you. You have to do the same thing in music, to obey the laws which are inherent in music. The difference is that you cannot say in words why this is an inherent law in music and why this is a grammatical law in language. You can prove the grammatical law. You cannot prove the inherent law of music. But we musicians feel it. So, you must excuse me, there are my limits.

What about jazz? What is your opinion about jazz?

Oh, don't provoke me! If you want to provoke me, then I feel I must answer, and I say that jazz is an insult to me. I feel debased by listening to it. I feel that the position of jazz in our music resembles in some way the position of the caricature and the cartoon in the graphic arts. There are very great talents for the cartoon and the caricature, but you would never compare it with great art in painting or in designing and so on. I only can say that jazz is a danger because it appeals to the lower instincts of the listener, and this is characteristic of some tendency in our time which I only can regret.

I gather from your remarks about jazz that you ascribe a certain moral force to music.

I do. Certainly. I even wrote about it. I am so sure of the moral quality in music because my whole life has taught it to me. The real proof for the high and lofty quality in music itself, as an element, lies in the fact that with religious works—*St Matthew Passion*, the *Missa Solemnis* of Beethoven, the *Messiah* of Handel—nobody will ever be astonished that they have been composed, because everybody must feel that the religious content of the words and the religious content of the music fit together. Music brings to mankind a very solemn and lofty message, and this perhaps may explain the worldwide love for music.

Looking back at your long career in music, would you have any general observations to make about what it has all meant to you?

I have such an observation to make. I want to say, looking back, that my life has been a very rich one. I had to go through trouble, I had to go through some ordeals. But I had also much happiness. I had much enjoyment and a very high sense of it. And I had all my life through, from my childhood on, the blessing of music. So, looking back on my life, I can feel only a fullness of gratitude to the higher powers.

Beverly Hills, July 1958

Sir Adrian Boult

ROBERT CHESTERMAN: *Sir Adrian, Igor Stravinsky said recently that the status of the conductor today is out of all proportion to his use in terms of an orchestra. I wonder if you would agree or think him wholly in error?*

SIR ADRIAN BOULT: No, I'm afraid perhaps I feel more strongly than he does. I should like all conductors to be clad in an invisible *Tarnhelm* which makes it possible to enjoy the music without seeing any of the antics that go on on platforms and which I deplore very much. I'm afraid I feel that at least nine-tenths of my colleagues on the platform of the Royal Festival Hall overdo it badly, and in overdoing it they simply put off the people they are supposed to be stimulating and inspiring and guiding.

How long, Sir Adrian, is it since you began conducting?

Oh, that wants some thinking about. I don't think I ever conducted anything except a composition of my own at about the age of eleven with a few long-suffering friends and my mother and sister. That was a nonet, I think, which I had composed and which didn't go very well, naturally; otherwise, I don't think I touched anything in the nature of conducting until I got to Oxford. Oh, I beg your pardon. At school we had inter-house singing competitions and I think I was responsible for one or two of those. But I am not sure that I did much conducting there. I think I was usually singing and I just wagged a finger occasionally when people had to take breaths together or finish together, or something of that kind.

I read somewhere that you wanted to conduct since you were a boy. I wondered if this was accurate?

Well, it is and it isn't. I was asked that question the other day—when I made up my mind I wanted to be a conductor—and I put it somewhere about sixteen or seventeen. My wife jumped down my throat and said it was more like two or three! I did show, I'm afraid, awful signs of precocity at that kind of age. I know I could read music before I could read print, and sundry things like that. But I believe that my first efforts at conducting were said to be at the back of a box in the Philharmonic Hall, Liverpool, when Hans Richter was on the platform. I did my best to copy him and was pushed into the background by my family. I know they said it had flummoxed me a bit when he got to the second movement of Tchaikovsky's *Pathétique* Symphony and I found five in a bar rather difficult to compass! That's the story, but I'm afraid I can't promise the truth of it!

You mentioned Liverpool. Where actually were you born?

I was born in Chester. My father was a businessman in Liverpool and we lived in the neighbourhood of Liverpool until he retired, which was after the 1914 war when I was getting on for thirty.

Your parents were musical, weren't they?

My father was very fond of it, but my mother was more than that. In fact, she was a very delicate woman and she might, if she'd been stronger—and of course had not married—have been a professional pianist.

When you went to school, you went to Westminster in London. How did that come about?

Oh, several reasons. First of all, my mother at that time, being a Southerner, was getting really rather fed up with life in a suburb of Liverpool. She longed for a little flat in London, where she could go and see pictures and hear music and so on. I was terribly overgrown. I was this height when I was fifteen, and it was considered at that time—1901 or so—not very wise to send a creature like that to a boarding school. And so a little flat was taken just on the south side of Westminster Bridge. I could trot across to school every day and went to Westminster as a day boy. And that turned out to be the most wonderfully successful thing for me. There was very little music at school, but I was given season tickets for Sir Henry Wood's two main series, the Sunday concerts and the Saturday afternoon symphony concerts. I went regularly to those, and naturally by the time I was eighteen I'd accumulated a pretty good repertoire—by knowledge, by hearing.

Can you remember the soloists and the conductors you heard in those days?

Oh yes, of course. Before school I had been nurtured mainly on Richter. I heard the greater classics all done by him, first of all. And then at the age of twelve I came into the orbit of Sir Henry Wood and heard a very great deal.

One of my first memories was Debussy conducting at one of the symphony concerts, and then soon after I went to school Arthur Nikisch, as Henry Wood's guest, conducted at one of the London Musical Festival concerts. I think that was Easter, 1903. He made a profound impression on me. Then, a year or two later, the London Symphony Orchestra was formed. That came about when Sir Henry Wood decided not to allow deputies at any of his concerts and the best players struck off and formed the London Symphony Orchestra. And they started off with an incredible list: Richter conducted five or six evening concerts; Nikisch, Steinbach, Weingartner, Peter Raabe and, I think, Vassily Safonov were all conductors of the first two or three seasons. This idea of guest conducting was a new one then, of course, and the whole thing excited us immensely. I went to as many of the LSO concerts as I possibly could in addition to my regular visits to the Sir Henry Wood concerts.

I know that English schoolboys, I think even to this day, are always expected to like games and sport, but never music. I wonder if you have any recollections along this line?

Well, there wasn't much music at school. We used to have a cheerful annual school concert when Gilbert and Sullivan operas or portions of them were bawled out. I'm quite certain that very few people ever sang the tenor or the bass parts of those operas; they all sang the tune an octave lower. That was the kind of standard we had. But, as I say, I had wonderful opportunities Saturdays and Sundays going to Queen's Hall and getting my fill. But one Saturday I remember I was just putting my books into my locker at the end of morning school and a big heavy voice behind me said, 'Well, young man, what are you going to do this afternoon?' Like an idiot I replied, with some pride, that I was going to Queen's Hall to hear Beethoven's Ninth Symphony for the first time. 'No, you're not, young fellow. You're going upfield to see the School beat Charterhouse!' Terrified, of course I did what I was told and I didn't hear the Ninth Symphony until a number of years later.

Have you seen the gentleman since that time and does he recall the incident?

He doesn't recall it, but I do! He used to come to Old Westminster gatherings sometimes and always ostentatiously talk music to me. He was a good deal older than I was and I never had the courage to bring that story back to him; but I wish I had now.

Did you commit scores to your memory by the time you were in your late teens?

Yes, I had a pretty good collection of miniature scores and I think I knew a good many of them by heart by the time I'd got to Oxford. It was my principal interest outside school work, of course.

When you were at Oxford you sang a lot, didn't you, in choirs?

Yes, I had a great deal of fun in all kinds of ways. And so much so that after a year Sir Hugh Allen advised me to give up any idea of an honours degree and just do the minimum to get a pass degree; and, of course, to take a musical degree in my fourth year.

You actually rowed for Christchurch at one time, didn't you?

Not for the college, not in the first Eight. I was in the college second Eight for two years and I rowed in a second Four at Henley in my last year. But I was never any good really. I think my back was too long. People are kind enough to say that I've got the longest back in Europe.

Earlier you mentioned Debussy conducting. Some commentators have recorded that Debussy really didn't conduct his own music all that well.

Well, the question of how composers conduct their own works is a very big one, isn't it? And very vexing! I remember Debussy conducting with a good deal of elbow and in his hand a rather ponderous club which was . . . well, to say it was like a rolled-up umbrella is rather an exaggeration, but it was that kind of fat thing and looking like anything but the ethereal loveliness of things like *L'Après-Midi d'un Faune* or the three Nocturnes. But the result that came out was absolutely magical. And that experience rather knocks the bottom out of all that I do and preach in the way of conducting techniques!

When Weingartner conducted in those days, was he conducting the Beethoven scores that he used to edit himself?

Now you're asking. I wouldn't know, because I didn't know the book in those days. But I must tell you a little about that book. The last time

Weingartner came to London he met a friend of mine, Herbert Menges, the conductor, and Menges asked him some question about the re-scoring of Beethoven. This is what Weingartner said: 'My friend, you have my book on the re-scoring of Beethoven. Please, will you do me a kindness? Go straight home, pick that book off the shelf and put it in the waste-paper basket.' Weingartner, in his profound maturity, had discovered that Beethoven knew better and knew best most of the time. That's a very nice reflection of the wonderful integrity of Weingartner's whole life and artistic output.

How many instruments did you learn to play in those early years?

I suppose I might say all or none. Beyond the piano, I never had a long series of lessons on any other instrument. I should have done, but somehow or other it seemed to be crowded out. But I was able at that time to get a contact with a man who was a very good all-round musician. He played first violin in the Liverpool Philharmonic Orchestra and was also conductor of the Liverpool City Police Band. We had our lessons at the police headquarters. I would spend a number of weeks on one instrument until I had got the fingering and was able to make the necessary noises and had an understanding of the instrument before we went on to another. It was a very wonderful lesson for me. I think I may say that I had a nodding acquaintance that way with every instrument in the orchestra.

You've written of this necessity in your book Thoughts on Conducting.

Yes, I've gone a very long way there, because I feel that what I did was really touching the fringe of it. I feel very strongly that nowadays, with the tremendous competition, people must be very much better equipped for the job than I was myself at that time.

After Oxford you went to the Leipzig Conservatory. Can you remember what year that was?

I was twenty-two and so that would be 1912.

It was here that you came very strongly in contact with Arthur Nikisch. You've written in a very concentrated manner about Nikisch. Of all the conductors that you heard, did you admire him the most?

Yes. I admired in him not so much his musicianship but his amazing power of saying what he wanted with a bit of wood. His power over the stick was quite unequalled by any conductor in my knowledge; so much so that his rehearsals were incredibly short always. He spoke very little, because almost all of it had been shown by the beautiful and expressive gestures that he made with his stick. That, I feel, is one objective which should be in the mind of every conductor.

As I've indicated, it is possible to say that conducting technique doesn't matter at all if you've got the concentration and you choose to look as Debussy looked conducting and can produce the sounds that Debussy could produce. But that, in a sense, is true of Toscanini. Because some of Toscanini's most wonderful pianissimos would come when his arm was swinging in such a way that, if he had been a pupil of mine, he'd have had it in the neck! He was making much too violent a gesture to get what I would think would be the gesture that would be easiest for the players to understand. No, I do feel that there is this reservation about technique. But at the same time I try and make all my pupils realize what can be done by a really beautiful flexible stick that will express what they want without their having to talk a lot about it.

Do you think that Nikisch was actually greater than Toscanini, or do you think that one should not make comparisons of this type?

Well, they've all got their own points of greatness. In my wildest moments I used to feel that Nikisch, with all the power and excitement that he generated, was not musically the master of anything like such a long list of works as quite a number of other conductors. In fact, I remember I used to say at that time that if you asked me to write a list of the works I would rather hear Nikisch conduct than any other conductor, it would be a shortish list: Weber overtures, Liszt, composers of that kind. But if it was Brahms, you would have a chance of a finer performance from a person like Steinbach, who knew Brahms intimately and had a great deal to do with the composition of some of his work. Tchaikovsky even, which Nikisch of course did marvellously, was somehow interpreted in a more strong and masculine manner by Vassily Safonov. With any composer, apart from certain exceptions, you could find somebody who was greater. For instance, in Wagner, if I wanted to hear a perfect performance of *Die Meistersinger* I would certainly have sent for Hans Richter. If I'd wanted a perfect performance of *Tristan* I would probably have said that is Nikisch, absolutely his cup of tea. But from the rehearsal point of view, from the point of view of actual technical control over the orchestra, I know no one to match Nikisch.

You wrote in your book that Nikisch's hands rarely rose above the level of his face.

Yes, that was a point. I remember we had a very exciting performance of Brahms's C minor Symphony, and suddenly it occurred to me, when it was over and we were all shouting ourselves hoarse, that Nikisch's hands had never been above the level of his face. And if he'd stretched to arm's length the roof would have fallen in or there would have been an earthquake. It was quite a thing, that economy.

And that, of course, is another thing I preach until I'm tired to young people: they will not—and experienced conductors will not—remember that the player sits behind music which is almost perpendicular. He wants to see just over the top of that music the gestures which are going to guide him in his performance; he doesn't want to look miles away from the music he is reading to see what the conductor has to offer. Therefore, the smaller the range the conductor can keep inside for his gestures, the easier it will be for the player to follow him.

Toscanini, though, achieved his results by sheer concentration, didn't he?

Toscanini, of course, was not an extravagant conductor. His gestures were always well circumscribed, well inside a circle of that kind. But I always felt that with him there was a power of concentration which was greater than perhaps anyone else who has conducted at all. It was the kind of concentration one hears coming from orators like Gladstone. And it was through the fierceness, the power, of his mental picture of the sound he wanted that he was able to infect his players that way alone, just through his eyes, to get the results he wanted. And from a sensitive orchestra, of course, Toscanini also could get an enormous amount of result without saying a word. I remember the first rehearsal he had with the BBC Symphony Orchestra. He took the Brahms E minor first and in the middle movements he did not stop at all. He went right through the movement. He had so little to say.

Well, coming back to Nikisch, you have said that he exerted a great power over an orchestra which even Beecham couldn't rival. But you were actually a great admirer of Beecham as well, weren't you?

Yes. I was an admirer of Beecham's power over the orchestra. Of course, I didn't see eye to eye with him as regards a great deal of the way he did things. Beecham was a really remarkable performer of music that wasn't quite first-rate. In fact, he took rather a pride in saying how bad he thought Beethoven's Fifth Symphony was, and that kind of thing, and I'm afraid that I find it difficult to see that sort of thing as funny. I know Beecham did it with his tongue in his cheek as a puckish way of amusing himself and shocking other people. But, quite seriously, I find I can't agree with a great deal of Beecham's ideals. For instance, his publication of two or three Mozart symphonies with an enormous number of expression marks everywhere—I don't feel that is really what Mozart needs to make him beautiful. I think: leave it alone and just coach your players into playing it the right way. That seems to me a more natural way of treating that kind of music.

How does a conductor obtain the results he wants? Is it possible to sum it up?

It's not easy, is it? The conductor should have in his mind before he comes to rehearsal an exact mental picture of what he wants to hear. He should then, in my view, not stop and break off the moment there is any divergence from that. Nikisch would very rarely stop an orchestra on the first reading through of anything; he would read right through to the end. He would then perhaps sum up in a few words, or make two or three points, where the performance that he'd just heard separated itself from the ideal performance that he'd had in his head beforehand. He would then show by a few general criticisms how the whole performance should be changed with regard to those points. He would then perhaps develop one or two of those points—the places where it showed most—and then he would probably, if he'd got a really intelligent orchestra and perhaps not too much time to rehearse, ask them to apply those points to other places and perhaps indicate one or two places where the same kind of treatment would help. He would leave it at that. Of course, if he had a second or third rehearsal he would cover it at the subsequent rehearsal. But he would be very careful not to labour a point more than adequately in that way, to stimulate the players to think for themselves along the lines he indicated for them. I was always struck by the sense of proportion in his rehearsing.

Let's go to the opposite pole for a moment. I remember a visitor at Liverpool. He had something really tough like Respighi's *Pines of Rome* to do, and I think two short concertos, and Beethoven's Fifth Symphony. Well, of course, I would suggest that if you have got a programme of that kind the first thing you'd do would be to break the back of *Pines of Rome*. To begin with, that would be the most sensible thing to do because that is for the largest orchestra of anything in that programme. Not so this little friend. He began with Beethoven's Fifth Symphony. He had two rehearsals of three hours and, having had one whole rehearsal and an hour of the next, he got near the end of the Beethoven when somebody reminded him that he'd got all the rest to do. He tore his hair and rushed out of the room, which didn't contribute very much to further rehearsal for that programme. However, it went over somehow.

Bruno Walter used to speak of the human and spiritual qualities of a conductor. He said that if a man does not love nature and the brook, he never could conduct the Pastoral *Symphony of Beethoven. I wonder if you find these sympathies very Viennese?*

Oh yes, how true. Walter was a wonderful friend and a wonderful conductor in every way. In fact, one of the greatest I've ever met, and it was a great privilege to hear him talk about everything, and I'm sure I wouldn't dream of disagreeing with an axiom of that kind. Some people used to say he over-sentimentalized his Mozart. I didn't find it really; I always found it very agreeable and lovely. But there are so many different ways and, personally, I am rather inclined to go for the middle line and steer a middle course—a British compromise and all that, I suppose.

Nowadays, it does seem that the cult of the personality is at its height. It seems that for a young person coming up, if he has the right attributes that are attractive to the general wherewithal of radio and television and the mass media, that this does assume too great a sway and does not take enough note of his musical abilities. Are you ever struck by this at all yourself?

Well, unfortunately it's become a commonplace, hasn't it, that the prima donna conductor is now in the twentieth century where the prima donna singer was in the nineteenth? There it is; and I think it's a lot of nonsense. Of course, it's encouraged by a great many of our colleagues. But I think it does a lot of harm really to cultivate the personality as against the music. After all, the conductor is the servant of the composer, and the greatest conductors I've known, Toscanini and Bruno Walter—I've heard them both talking about composition—spoke with veneration of the Beethovens and the Mozarts who'd suffered so much to give them this wonderful music to recreate and recreate. I think anyone who's had the privilege of hearing people like that talk about their work cannot fail to despise the protagonists of the modern attitude. No, I'm all against it, I'm afraid.

Do you think quality will always win out in the long run, that the younger conductor with the great talent will come to the fore?

It's an awfully difficult question to answer. One does know how opportunity has come to some people and brought them to the front, perhaps more quickly than one would think they deserve. Other people, who are doing sterling work, are left behind because they haven't perhaps quite enough of the glamour to affect this, as you say, personality-minded generation. Somehow I like to feel that real worth will get through in the end. But, there's no question about it, it takes a good deal longer if one has not had that kind of opportunity. One feels terribly sorry for people who just miss the finest rewards even though they've got the right point of view.

Surely it takes years, though, before a conductor can have the necessary experience to really effect what he wants?

That is quite true. I think the most unfortunate thing about these international competitions is that they are keeping their age limits so low. They should have it up to forty or forty-five, in my opinion.

What do you say to people who must, I am sure, come up to you from time to time and say, 'I want my boy to become a conductor; what does he have to do?'

I would say, 'Look for another profession!' That's my first answer! In the preface to my book I try and list all the qualifications there. I think I say at the end that nobody I know can fulfil all the qualifications, but most of them every young conductor should be master of. Maybe the alternative is musical suicide. A person who wants to become a musician must contemplate an alternative, and if, in contemplating that alternative, they say, 'I'd rather put my head into a gas oven,' well then there's no hope except going in for music; otherwise I'd say take the other thing.

I had a very delightful letter, a good many years ago now, from a young man who said, 'You won't remember, but I asked your advice about a musical career. I was very keen about it and my uncle had just offered me a nice position with him in his factory, and you told me

decisively to go to my uncle, and I did. That was seven years ago. The
uncle has now retired and I'm in charge of the business. I think it's of
great interest and I'm enjoying it very much and, in addition, on
Monday I sing in the so-and-so choral society, on Tuesday I act in the
so-and-so amateur operatic society, on Wednesday I play the violin in
the so-and-so orchestral society, and so on.' Now, wasn't that chap
getting as much out of music, when music was his servant in that way,
as he might have done unless he'd been absolutely at the very top of the
professional tree? So I say avoid music if you possibly can find an
alternative.

*Sir Adrian, I'd like to turn to orchestras generally. To what extent do you
think an orchestra adds an expressiveness of its own to an interpretation?*

I've noticed it in all kinds of ways. At conductor competitions sometimes you'll find even a young conductor will affect tone at once in
two bars. It will be entirely different. I remember Egon Wellesz, when
he was a critic in Vienna, talking about an orchestra. I was asking how
some young English conductor got on with the Vienna Philharmonic.
'Oh,' he said, 'any conductor who doesn't disturb the Vienna Philharmonic gets on quite well with it.' I thought not only was that a very
good remark in itself, but it was a wonderful definition of a great
orchestra. I determined that, if ever I had charge of an orchestra
myself, I would see that, unless disturbed, it could play well.

I remember a very interesting remark that was made by an anony-
mous critic in a London paper somewhere in the early years of the
century. Richter and Nikisch both conducted the *Flying Dutchman*
overture in the same hall with the same orchestra a night or two apart.
What he said was this: 'With Nikisch we felt that fate was pursuing us
wherever we went; with Richter fate was facing us wherever we
turned.' That answers your question of how an orchestra can change,
how the same body of people can convey an utterly different slant, an
utterly different tendency, about the same music if a different man is
in charge of them. The power of the conductor of the orchestra is . . .
well, it's the greatest mystery of one's life, isn't it? One can't define
it at all.

*You've just returned from America, where you've been conducting the Boston
Symphony Orchestra at Tanglewood in their annual festival. Do you find a great
difference between an American orchestra and a British orchestra?*

Well, as one hears them, one knows how the London critics always go for the streamlining, the perfection, the ensemble perfection of American orchestras, and then they show the other side of the medal and perhaps there isn't quite so much interpretative interest, interpretative beauty about it. But I must say I did not find that at all weak in the Boston orchestra's performance. Of course, I was doing a Mozart programme and I did precious little to it. I left them alone and I thought the playing was very lovely indeed.

There's no difference in standard, but a difference in kind?

Yes. Of course Boston is, perhaps from the nature of its work and the people who've been in charge of it, less American than some of the other American orchestras. But I certainly found nothing offensive in their treatment of Mozart, nothing mechanical, nothing metallic, shall I say, about it.

With your tremendous experience over the years, I wonder if you find the general standard of playing actually higher now than it was, say, thirty years ago?

Quite incredibly. Perhaps I can tell you the story of the early BBC orchestra which was formed, as you'll remember, in 1930. The recruiting of it was done in two ways. The leading desks were recruited, of course, from the greatest players you could find all over the country. The back desks of the strings were recruited in quite a different way. Great players like Albert Sammons and Lionel Tertis were sent to provincial places, and they spent two or three days in Glasgow, Belfast, and so on, hearing players, and brought back a number of untried new young people.

Soon after the orchestra was formed, I suggested that we should do a complete act of Wagner at a symphony concert. This was approved and I decided on the last act of *Siegfried* and engaged two big soloists to take part in it. We then got to work. I said we must have an extra string rehearsal—I know what the Wagner string passages are. So we had our extra string rehearsal of three hours. The whole lot of passages, as we came to them, and which were played by these young people, came off instantly. I packed up the rehearsal after about an hour; there was nothing to rehearse.

Curiously enough, a few days after that, a very respected elderly member of one of the London orchestras came for an audition to join the BBC Symphony Orchestra. And at the so-called sight test we sat

him down to the last page of the first violin part of the *Götterdämmerung*
of Wagner. And I sat back, thinking I should hear the arpeggios and
perhaps find the intonation not quite perfect. But I assure you I
couldn't tell what the arpeggios were. I couldn't tell where he was in
the thing. He went on scratching up and down these streams of notes
and it was so out of tune that I didn't know what chords he was playing.
And this man had played the work with Richter year after year at
Covent Garden! He was a man, I suppose, of about fifty-five, compared
with the twenty-year-olds that we were glad to see in the BBC Symphony Orchestra.

You said it was 1930 that the BBC Symphony Orchestra came together?

There is a certain misconception about this, so perhaps you will
allow me to say a word with absolute accuracy. I was appointed
Director of Music for the BBC on 1st January, 1930. I didn't function
fully until the middle of that year, for a number of reasons, by which
time the whole plan of the BBC orchestra had been hatched and carried
out. Everything was settled before I got there and I may take no credit
at all for the recruiting of the orchestra. I might say almost all the best
players in the country had been earmarked by the BBC staff and my
predecessor, Mr Percy Pitt. The rank and file recruiting was done as
I've explained.

The first concert took place in October of 1930. The programme was
the overture to *The Flying Dutchman,* the Saint-Saëns Cello Concerto,
played by Suggia—who was then at the top of her form—and Brahms's
Fourth Symphony. We finished with the closing scene of Ravel's
Daphnis and Chloë, a work that had hardly been heard in London at that
time and made rather a sensation. At the end of that first season, at
which I had been privileged to conduct rather less than half the
concerts, Sir John Reith sent for me and said, 'Everybody tells me that
the orchestra plays better for you than for anyone else. Will you please
become its permanent conductor?' Of course I said I would be proud
and happy to do so. I was for eight years both Director of Music and
conductor of the orchestra, and I was very glad to retire to become
wholly a musician and not to bother about administrative matters at
the end of that time.

*There was tremendous opposition in the early 1930s to the idea of broadcast
concerts, was there not?*

Reith summoned a meeting to get advice on the problem. I believe it was attended by Sir Henry Wood, Sir Landon Ronald and Sir Thomas Beecham. I was invited, but unable to attend. There had been strong pressure on the BBC to agree at once that the new orchestra should be restricted to the studio and should give no public concerts. I believe the reply was voiced, principally by Sir Landon Ronald, that if the orchestra was restricted to the studio it would probably go out of existence before it was two years old. They said the players would be bored stiff always playing in the studio and they must have the stimulus of a public concert, or they would become a second-rate orchestra. And that was the choice.

And you felt this way yourself?

Now you're asking! I think I did feel that way, really because so many eminent people had said the same thing. But, personally, I still feel I shouldn't mind facing a future that was restricted to the studio. I liked to see that red light go on and picture my old father sitting in his armchair and a number of other friends listening in their rooms. I did not really feel that I needed the stimulus of the public. But perhaps I am a bit of a freak about that kind of thing.

Did you introduce many new works with the BBC Symphony?

Oh, we did. Edward Clark on the BBC staff had a close friendship with everybody. We would say, 'Well, Edward, what's happening in the Stravinsky world now?' And he would tell us. And the same with Schoenberg and all the Viennese School. Of course, where Stravinsky was concerned we usually got Ansermet over to do them for us.

Did you conduct Schoenberg and Webern at all?

Yes. I remember we did the Schoenberg Variations somewhere about the second or third season with the orchestra, and later we did the first public performance in Vienna. Somebody had discovered they'd only been given in a studio performance.

What was the reaction?

Mild horror from the ordinary classical-loving Viennese audience, I'm afraid. I remember the Federal President of Austria asked me to his box in the interval and looked at me very suspiciously. He said, 'Who is this Schoenberg anyway?'

Did you enjoy conducting this music?

No, I can't say I leapt at modern music as some people do. I found a tremendous craftsman's interest in turning the thing into sound as the composer had envisaged. But I can't say I enjoyed the music as such. I was usually happier with a Brahms symphony. But perhaps the exception I may make to that was the opera *Wozzeck*, which we had rehearsed very carefully for a long time; it had a completely English cast, which was coached for three months by a young répétiteur from Berlin. I still treasure a letter written by Berg himself after he heard it through Swiss Radio.

This is very interesting, for those who tend to associate you just with English music, to recall that you played a repertoire which extended well into the moderns.

Yes, I suppose that is true. I was asked the other day, 'Why do you never do Mahler and Bruckner in your programmes?' I very nearly answered, 'Because I did all of them before you were born!' But I framed it a little better than that. I think I may claim credit for doing Mahler right back in the twenties.

You did a tremendous amount of commercial recording in the thirties too, and I believe you were among the small group of pre-electric conductors, along with Sir Thomas Beecham.

I shall never forget meeting Holst at lunch at the College, where we usually met. He said, 'Adrian, I've just done my first recording and wasn't it extraordinary! There I was, perched up on a little seat high in the wall of the place, and I looked across and there were the horns turning their backs on me; and there was the poor solo violin sitting with his scroll inside a horn. It was all very funny indeed. And no double basses at all, just a tuba poppling along with the bass part!' Well, that was an extreme description of it, but it was that kind of thing. The horns literally did sit a long way away with their backs to you, looking at you in the looking-glass, so that the sound came out the right way!

How many recordings did you do along these lines?

Already in 1919 I had done a season of ballet with Diaghilev, and the first things I was asked to record by HMV were the Suite for the *Good-Humoured Ladies* ballet by Scarlatti and the Rossini *Boutique Fantasque*. Soon after we did Butterworth's *A Shropshire Lad*, which we did in a truncated version because everything had to be cut in those days.

One of the pieces you did in the 1920s with the British Symphony Orchestra was Arthur Bliss's Rout.

Yes, the British Symphony Orchestra was really the beginnings of the English Chamber Orchestra, that sort of thing. It was an orchestra of about twelve to sixteen players and we had a great time. Anne Thursfield was the singer, and we had this terrible contact business where you made your record and if there was a blemish on it you had to do it all again. We had finally got a good one, and just as it finished the composer, who was sitting in the studio, shouted out, 'By Jove, you fellows, that's splendid!' I said they ought to sell it like that. But we had to do it all again.

I wonder if you approve of all the developments that have taken place in the recording industry since that time?

One can only say that there are improvements. But I think they are being driven to an extreme length now in the way they patch. I always say to a new recording manager, 'Look, my job is to produce as fine a performance as I can, whole, for you. And it's your job to take it whole and put it on wax. If there are one or two blemishes, I'm prepared to make one or two patches for you, but I'd far rather not. And if there are more than two or three, we'll do it all again.' Because I think the spontaneity and continuity of a performance can very easily be wrecked.

Do you listen to the gramophone very much?

Not very much. You see, I was brought up before the days of the gramophone and the idea of studying a score to the gramophone somehow has never got under my skin. When I'm asked about studying in this way, I'm inclined to say that a student ought to have two or three records of the work and not get stereotyped into one performance of it. He should learn it from the paper if he cannot have these different performances. The student has got to get back to the work itself without going through anybody else's sieve, as it were.

What is the most difficult project you have ever undertaken in a recording studio?

My mind goes back to *Wozzeck*, but we didn't record that, of course.

We had quite a problem last week with *The Planets*. The final move-ment, 'Neptune', with its disappearing female choir, is a terrible problem for recording.

You conducted the first performance of The Planets. *Can you remember the circumstances now?*

Well, during the 1914 war *The Planets* was written. Holst wrote it just because he wanted to and he never thought he'd hear it. It was arranged for two pianos by two of his assistants, and that was how I was first introduced to it about the third or fourth year of the war.

One day in the late summer of 1918, when the war was getting near its end, he came to me very breathlessly, into my office, and said, 'Adrian, I've got some news. I've got to go to Salonika to entertain the troops, and Balfour Gardiner, bless his heart, has given me a parting present, and the parting present is Queen's Hall, full of the Queen's Hall Orchestra, for the whole of a Sunday morning, and we are going to do *The Planets* and you've got to conduct.' Well, I didn't know *The Planets* well enough to conduct. However, there were a few weeks left and St Paul's Girls' School turned to and spent a lot of time copying the parts. And as the parts were copied, each Planet was sent round to me to study.

The great day duly came. Sunday morning. The platform was full of the Queen's Hall Orchestra. The gallery was not occupied, but the balcony and stalls were very full of all his friends. He had a great many friends of course in the profession, and he had two or three generations of Paulines, girls from St Paul's Girls' School, who were all eager to come. They also organized the disappearing choir for 'Neptune'. I remember they sang at the back and walked out as the sound is supposed to disappear. We planned the three hours in the obvious way: we rehearsed from ten o'clock till about a quarter to twelve, then a little break, and then at twelve o'clock we started in and played the work right through. It made a great impression, naturally, with a thoroughly enthusiastic audience like that.

And that's how *The Planets* began. It was only a year or so later, somewhere about '21 or '22 I think, that they had their first full performance, conducted by Albert Coates in Queen's Hall, at which I had the pleasure to conduct the distant choir and organize the way the music disappears until you don't know whether you are hearing the thing in your ears or whether it really is the sound that's coming to you.

Do you think The Planets *is a complete masterpiece?*

Oh yes, I don't question it at all. Always, wherever I have done it, it has always been received as a work of tremendous importance and tremendous interest. And, of course, its message is so sharply divided; the seven movements all represent their particular tendency, and I think they exploit their tendency and display it in a masterly way.

Was Holst delighted with the success of the work?

Yes, up to a point. But he was a very realistic person and I remember a bit later, when somebody expressed the opinion to a friend of mine that he wanted to finance a Holst Festival, I was one of the go-betweens. I went to Gustav and he said, 'Oh yes, that's very nice, but I'm getting plenty of performances. What I want is time to write more.'

When you first conducted a large orchestra for the first time, was it what you expected? Or were you greeted with a barrage of sound from all sides?

No, I think I'd been fortunate enough by that time to have heard a very great deal of orchestral music, and to have heard it not only from the distance, the circle or whatever it was. No, I think my first concert with a professional orchestra went pretty well as I'd imagined it.

Do you remember the programme?

I remember, greatly daring, I did the Hugo Wolf *Italian Serenade*, which was not very well known to the orchestra. On one occasion, when the wind soloist—who was rather famed for being, shall we say, extremely Lancashire about things—came in a bar late, I told him so. He said, 'I've played this work a hundred times and I know I was right.' So I said, 'Very well, Mr X, we were all a bar early.' The orchestra cheered and I got my own back. It was very lucky to be presented with an opportunity like that at one's first meeting with a professional orchestra.

Do you always conduct with a score?

Yes, I always have it there. I don't always look at it. I don't necessarily turn it upside down, as Hans von Bülow is supposed to have done. But I like the feeling of the desk just there, just to my left hand with the spare stick. The desk with the score on it is part of my furniture. I am not one of those people who prefer to have no desk and so have the complete range. I don't want to conduct down by my knees at all; I like to have the desk there. In fact, sometimes in a strange hall, if I'm not quite sure how things are going, I place the desk as I want it. I then hold my hand above it. I ask if all the players can see my hand. And if any of them say they can't, I lift the desk a little to remind me to keep my hand up. I feel it's very important to have the field of work in easy sight of everybody, otherwise one has to behave like a windmill, which I don't like doing. I'm too lazy for that.

But works like the Beethoven Eighth you do conduct from memory, though, don't you?

Oh yes, but the score is always there.

Do you regard the score as holy writ, as something that should not be tampered with?

Well, going back to Weingartner and his amendments, I think there are only about two places in the whole of the Beethoven symphonies where I make any alteration. With Schumann, of course, one has to alter dynamics a certain amount because the things don't sound. I think perhaps I might say it's holy writ as regards the notes practically always. But as regards dynamics I think in many cases one can probably get a better result by marking the accompaniments down. I would very seldom mark the tunes up; I think that's a mistake. And with certain composers, notably Delius, I start in this way. I tell players to look on these dynamic signs as a general guide to what they do, but not to follow them slavishly. All the time there is something very beautiful going on, a tune somewhere probably or a progression of some kind, and they should listen for that all the time. I think that is a much better way of planning the whole fabric of the performance than messing about marking a lot of things.

Regarding the layout of an orchestra, you made quite a point in Thoughts on Conducting *about having the second violins on the right. Now when Norman del Mar reviewed your book he said he abandoned this formation early in his career and for purely practical reasons never dared to return to it. Yet you have actually persisted.*

I have persisted. I am very firm about it now. I used to give way if I was being a guest for a short time. For instance, in Boston last time I was there for three weeks and I left it alone. And I regretted it very much, because on many occasions we got answering passages first

against second violins, and the second violins sounding from the back
of the hall were just a pale reflection of the firsts. It didn't, in my view,
convey the composer's message at all. So I am now a good deal firmer
and I always ask for it.

Sometimes I make occasion with a fresh orchestra to apologize to the
leader of the second violins, because I know it puts a considerable strain
on them in regard to timing. I find that in more than nine cases out of
ten they welcome it as a challenge. They say they like to feel that they
are an entity on their own account. And I would like to add an almost
equally important thing to do with the basses. I had this proved by
several other people who remember Hans Richter had four basses in
one corner of his stage and four in the other, in order to have a balanced
background. And this idea of putting all the basses right down at the
right of the outfit—sometimes right at the front of the stage—would
have been absolute anathema to him. No, I think we must have our
strings properly balanced and then everything else will fall into place.

Are you conscious that your readings have changed a lot over the years?

No, I'm not really. I always try and feel that they're never stereotyped. The day after a performance, if I've got some time in a bus or
train or something, I shut my eyes and I go over the performance and
I see where I can improve points in it, and whether the overall balance
structure was properly conveyed. But I'm not conscious that there have
been many differences.

*Do you regard the rehearsal as a fixed indication of the performance that's
going to follow? Do you predict in your rehearsals exactly what's going to happen
in the performance?*

No, most definitely not. I know that is the way, mostly, it's done in
America and the way Toscanini used to do it in southern Europe at any
rate. Personally, I take rather the reverse view. I feel that I'm more
like the trainer, the athletic trainer, who's bringing the thing gradually
forward to, well, concert pitch is the wrong word, I suppose, but to the
point, let's say, of the Boat Race—and, after all, the Boat Race is the
maximum effort. No, I think the thing about the Anglo-Saxon orchestral
player, and I think the Scandinavian probably too, is that they like
being gradually brought to the pitch and then they will have something
more.

Furtwängler, of course, was noted in his performances for his improvising at the moment. Did you hear Furtwängler very much?

Oh yes, I heard him a good many times. I suppose the thing that struck anyone the first time about Furtwängler was the extraordinary apparent difficulty of following him and yet the fact that the ensemble was perfect. But I remember very well the very first time I heard him, in Vienna, with the Ninth Symphony. As the performance began I thought, 'Well, this is terrific.' The first crescendo, the first climax, was thundering and overpowering. I leant back and I thought to myself, 'How on earth is this man going to hold this performance together if he's got it like this on the first two or three pages?' He did hold it together and it was structurally in one piece. But the whole of the light on the detail was stronger than anything I'd ever experienced before. This was just after the First World War and I had been hearing rather second-rate performances, and that performance came as a great revelation to me.

You're obviously not a believer in the fact that the more rehearsals an orchestra has, the better it will be.

Certainly not. I feel that staleness is a thing that is very much neglected and much overlooked. A great many of my colleagues don't notice when their stuff is getting stale. It's as bad as that. This modern habit of having a rehearsal on the afternoon of the concert is, to me, a great mistake, and I always resist it if I can. If I've got to do it, I put as much rehearsal as I possibly can into the day before, to avoid having much to do on the day of the concert.

After a concert performance do you read criticisms in the newspapers of the performance?

Not so much now. I used to learn a very great deal. Perhaps it's not very kind to say so, but I find nowadays there are not many younger critics from whom I feel I can learn very much. On the other hand, when I was young and the critics were considerably older, I learnt a very great deal by reading very carefully.

You've conducted all kinds of music throughout your career, and I wonder what excites you most when you conduct now?

I find it awfully difficult to compare things at all. When I'm asked for my favourite Brahms symphony, I always say the one I'm working on.

Could I ask what factors make you decide to perform a new work?

I really am not very good at answering that, because I let non-musical factors have a great deal to do with it. In so many cases, through my twenty years at the BBC, a score has just been sent to me: 'Would you like to do this work?' Practically always I say yes. No, I'm afraid I can't enumerate the factors that make me think that a work is a great work and ought to be done. I believe in finding room for everything if I possibly can.

Finally, Sir Adrian, can I ask you, when you look back over the years, if there's anything that has really perturbed you at all in the musical world?

No, I don't think I can say. I'm not that sort of person, you see. I just take things as they come and do my best to make the best of them. I have my likes and dislikes, of course, but further than that I don't think I really can honestly go.

London, July 1966

Leonard Bernstein

ROBERT CHESTERMAN: *Mr Bernstein, it has been said that nothing surprises you, and I wonder now, as you look back to 1943 when you stepped in at the last moment for an ailing Bruno Walter, if you think that most conductors' major opportunities happen in this way—that the lucky break has to play a part?*

LEONARD BERNSTEIN: First of all, I would have to say that I am constantly surprised by everything! It's exactly the opposite of what you imply. My whole life has been a series of surprises. There is almost an occult factor when you think that everything began to happen suddenly in my life at my twenty-fifth birthday. Beginning with that specific day came a series of lucky chances that one reads about only in Horatio Alger novels, very bad novels in fact. In the years immediately preceding that moment when everything changed, I was in a state of despair. But I would say that luck did have a great deal to do with it. Of course, luck is no earthly use if you're not ready to take advantage of the occasion when it does arise.

If you are specifically prepared, for example, for that famous day when Bruno Walter unfortunately got sick and I had to take over at a couple of hours' notice without rehearsal. The programme was a very difficult one. But it was one that had intrigued me so that I had given a great deal of time to studying it, without any thought that I would be called upon to conduct it at such short notice. It included *Don Quixote* of Strauss, which is a piece I hadn't known, and I just fell in love with it and, in particular, with the way Strauss handled the literary and philosophical allusions; this led me to a very detailed study of the piece. I didn't just prepare myself to be able to get through it if an emergency arose. I went much further than that. I remember being up nights that week with the score, revelling in it and re-reading Cervantes and making comparisons with the literary original, so that when this thing did happen on the Sunday morning I was more than superficially prepared with *Don Quixote*—in a way that enabled me to give more than a skin-deep performance. I don't mean to be boastful about it, but in spite of my tremendous case of nerves, which I had, and excitement and fear and anxiety about this whole thing, I was able to lose myself in this score to a degree that I wouldn't have been able to do had I not been sufficiently prepared.

When you speak of surprises, I'm surprised every morning when I get up that I'm there and that there is a world around me still going on. I think that without this element of surprise I would not be able to maintain the enthusiasm for life and art that I have. Life is an enormous list of surprises and the day I cease being surprised I shall quit, because I won't be much good, I'm afraid. I was certainly surprised about that day, 14th November, 1943, and the reason I use the word 'occult' in connection with it is that these things always seem to fall either in terms of particular dates which have concomitant meanings, or else around numbers that are somehow attached. One could almost become an astrologer or numerologist addict when some of these are examined. I can't go into all of them because they would bore you to tears.

The fact is that on my twenty-fifth birthday, which happens to fall on 25th August, I was in a state of extreme despair because I had just been rejected for the second time by the army on the grounds of asthma. I had a job which I just loathed, which had to do with making transcriptions in the world of jazz and commercial music at a jazz publishing firm, for which I received $25 a week. I couldn't seem to get anything else. I had graduated from Harvard and from the Curtis Institute by that time. I had studied two years with Fritz Reiner. I had studied three summers, from 1940 to 1942, with Koussevitzky at Tanglewood. I was presumably ready to conduct, to play the piano, to have my compositions heard, and nothing was happening at all. To top it all off, even the army didn't want me. I was of no use to anyone.

I was just about to drown myself in the river on the 25th August, 1943, when I received a telephone call that very day. I had just returned from Boston—where the draft board rejected me—to the Berkshire Music Center. It was from a man called Artur Rodzinski, whom I'd never met but naturally knew about. He was a very well-known conductor who had been the conductor of the Cleveland Symphony, and formerly of the Los Angeles Orchestra. He had a farm in Stockbridge, which was a nearby town. He asked me if I would come and see him at his farm, which I did. He met me. It was all very mysterious, like an Antonioni movie. I went into this farm and a man on a motor scooter with a beekeeper's helmet on his head approached. I really thought I was on Mars or somewhere. And this man was Rodzinski. He greeted me and took me to a haystack in which we sat. He said, 'As you know'—which I didn't know—'I have just been appointed conductor of the New York Philharmonic and I start next month, September.' I said, 'Congratulations.' And he said, 'I need a conductor. I have not been sure who to take or whether to retain the present incumbent. So I asked God whom I should take and God said take Bernstein. And so I've called you and will you take the job?'

Of course, by this time, what with the beekeeping helmet and the scooter, and the haystack, and this unbelievable, volcanic statement, my jaw was dropped a foot and a half. I couldn't believe what I was hearing, but did summon up the energy to say, 'Yes. Thank you.' We shook on it. I didn't ask any further questions. I didn't ask him how he happened to have a direct wire to God. I just bought it as it was. It later turned out that the direct wire to God existed apropos his belonging to the Oxford Movement, the Buchmanite Group, which does talk to God regularly. It seems it all had to do in his case with the surrendering of the ego, which apparently was one of his severe problems, and becoming one with God. For this I've been very grateful to God ever since, as you can imagine.

Then it goes on, because once I was there, installed in my little one-room apartment in Carnegie Hall, which was a mansion compared with where I'd been living, I was just thrilled at making $125 a week as assistant conductor of the Philharmonic, which was an amazing amount of money to me. I couldn't have been happier. I proceeded to do my duties, which were to study all the scores, be ready in case Rodzinski were sick or, if a guest conductor became indisposed, to take over a rehearsal or indeed a concert. Of course, there's a strong tradition in the conducting world that conductors almost never get sick, and I believe no conductor had become indisposed at the Philharmonic for something like fifteen years. Therefore I was ready to accept the fact that it was never going to happen.

But it did happen. I'd been there exactly two months. Bruno Walter was the guest conductor and he did indeed get sick, and indeed it was that programme of *Don Quixote*, and indeed it was a nationwide broadcast on a Sunday afternoon, which made it all the more exciting and fantastic. I don't know why it means so much to me, but the 14th of November was already an important date because it was Aaron Copland's birthday. That it should all happen on that day supplies again a kind of magic touch.

Why is it that native-born conductors have it so hard in America?

I don't think they do any more, but they certainly did then. I mean, at that point, without an accent and a beard, and being of the age I was, nobody was interested at all.

As a matter of fact, a couple of months after that Rodzinski himself got sick. But at that time I couldn't take over for him because I had a previous contract with the Pittsburgh Symphony to go down and play the world première of my first symphony, *Jeremiah,* at Fritz Reiner's request. He very kindly and very generously asked me to come down and conduct this work, which had never been heard. It was my first orchestral piece and he believed in it. And that was a wild success also; in fact, I've never seen a review of a new work on the front page banner headline in a major city. It also won the music critics' prize that year. In the same season, my first ballet which I had been working on, *Fancy Free,* saw the light of day at the Metropolitan Opera House. You can't really look at a period like that without believing a little bit in some sort of astrological force. Then in the same year of '44 I wrote *On the Town,* which was my first Broadway show, and that opened in December and was an enormous success also.

You mentioned Koussevitzky. He was your mentor?

He was not my first mentor. My first was Fritz Reiner. There was a great deal of difference between the approach of these two men, the difference, I would say, between the South Pole and the North Pole. That's one of the things I was very lucky in too, to have two teachers who so complemented each other and were so different, from each of whom I got so much fresh material and approach to conducting.

- For example, Reiner was a very severe teacher and a severe technician. His standards were enormously high on knowledge, on knowing every score. You simply do not ascend that podium unless you know everything you can know about the score at that moment. You have to have the right to conduct. He was extremely interested in stick movement. He used a very large baton. He used it very minutely; his beats were almost microscopic. But they were incredibly forceful and magnetic. I still don't know quite how he achieved it. He was very economical in his beating, in his gesture; he almost never gave up-beats to begin a piece. He would rely on the orchestra to come with his down-beat. He would scare them into it. And it almost always worked when he had a good orchestra. I'll never forget his beginning *Don Juan* of Strauss, which is a very tricky beginning and usually demands a very clear up-beat before giving the down-beat, just after which the orchestra enters. He never gave an up-beat. The stick would just drop, tick, and the orchestra would be there. I never knew how. I never knew what made them be together. A miracle.

Koussevitzky was the opposite. Very careful up-beats, but not very clear down-beats. Very different from this technical approach. He was what one might describe as an inspirational kind of teacher. His whole approach to conducting came from the emotions. As he would put it, 'The varmth, it must be like the sun, the legato, the vunderful line.' It was very moving and very exciting to study with him. But it was the exact reverse from studying with Reiner.

Klemperer has said that 'mostly one conducts with the eyes'. Would you agree?

That was very true of both Reiner and Koussevitzky. As a matter of fact, I think Reiner did much more with the eyes than with the stick. I remember his eyes peering like arrows at the orchestra over his little half-glasses, nailing them to him, magnetizing them, so that this little movement of the stick would accomplish that. Koussevitzky also had tremendous magnetism with his eyes. I don't know about me because I've never seen myself. I don't know what I do. I haven't the vaguest idea what I do on the podium, so I can't tell you anything about myself.

I'd like to ask you about your time with the New York Philharmonic. Is it possible to sum up what you feel you have achieved in the sense of a performing ensemble since you took over the orchestra?

Well now, that is a very large question. What have we achieved, since I took over the orchestra? Let me start a little obliquely by saying that there is another conductor who was also a mentor and who had an enormous influence on me, and that's Dimitri Mitropoulos. As a matter of fact, I knew him before I knew either Reiner or Koussevitzky. He came to Boston as a guest conductor while I was still at Harvard and I met him. This is also a great set of occult circumstances, and I won't go into them because they're too long, but it really is quite scary.

I met him at a tea which was given at Harvard in the Phillips Brooks house by the Greek Society at Harvard, which was known as the Helicon Society. He, being a famous Greek, was entertained by this Society. I had not thought of going to it, but at the last minute I did, for reasons I don't know. There was a long line of people waiting to shake hands with Mitropoulos. There was music played in his honour, tea was served, and I was just one of this long line. When I met him, he asked me what I did at Harvard and I told him I was a musician. He asked me to play the piano for him, which I did, with very sweaty palms. He decided forthwith that I was someone that he considered special musically. He used very extravagant language, words like 'genius-boy' and so on. I was just overwhelmed. I had never thought of myself as anything of the sort. He invited me to attend the rehearsals of the Boston Symphony that week and I went to every one. I had lunch with him one day. He gave me a signed picture and left. That was our relationship.

But I happened to run into him some years later, as a matter of fact just after my graduation from Harvard, when I was again in a period of despair. I couldn't get a job and I'd never thought of conducting all the time I was at Harvard and I ran into him by sheer accident. I told him my troubles and Dimitri said, 'You must be a conductor.' 'What makes you say that?' I said, 'You've never seen me conduct.' 'I don't have to,' 'Well,' I said, 'how does one become a conductor? I'll do anything at this point.' I had just spent a whole summer looking for a job in New York and failed. He told me to try the Juilliard School. But it was too late to apply. And then he told me to try the Curtis Institute —'Fritz Reiner teaches there in Philadelphia.' I did, and found to my amazement that they were accepting applications in spite of the lateness of the season, because Reiner had been delayed by European engagements and he hadn't formed his class yet. I went down there for an audition and was accepted, again to my amazement, because I had never conducted or really studied scores from a conductorial point of view, only from a composer's point of view or a student's point of view. So I was suddenly a pupil of Fritz Reiner. And I owe this to Dimitri, who first suggested to me that I ought to be a conductor.

As of this moment I had not yet met Koussevitzky. Imagine, I had lived in Boston all that time and attended the Boston Symphony concerts, and I had never met him.

Mitropoulos was also influential in my memory of his conducting—the conducting itself, the way he conducted. I was terribly impressed in that series of rehearsals where I had observed him in Boston. He was like a wild man. He jumped and crouched, knew everything by heart. He had perhaps the most phenomenal memory in history, a photographic memory. He rushed down into the violas, in among them, gesticulating madly. The orchestra adored him, the audience adored him, and it was a week of incredible music-making. I'll never forget it and the influence still remains with me.

The reason I began the answer to that question about the New York Philharmonic so obliquely is because Dimitri later became the conductor of the New York Philharmonic and I succeeded him. Mitropoulos did extraordinary things during his tenure with the New York Philharmonic for the repertoire, for young and new composers. But he also left the orchestra in what I must confess was rather a ragged state, because he was terribly interested in the dynamics of music and in a dynamic repertoire, but he was not terribly interested in the actual sound an orchestra made, as long as they gave him the accents and the pianissimos, the bold dynamic outlines of a piece. He didn't really care very much whether it was in tune, really in tune, or about the various refinements of bowing—whether you bowed with the tip or at the frog or up or down or with more weight or less. The orchestra, especially in Mozart or Beethoven, had begun to sound quite coarse with him. He wasn't really interested in Mozart and Beethoven. As he confided to me in a personal conversation, he had grown to a point where this was kind of dull because it didn't challenge him enough. He wanted to conduct Schoenberg, and the Schnabel Symphony, and anything that was long, arduous and very complicated, and preferably dodecaphonic. I think he missed a very big point there, which is that there is nothing in the world more challenging than to conduct eight bars of Mozart, that it's much easier to conduct eight hundred bars of Schoenberg.

You obviously think the classical repertoire makes the more total demands on a conductor.

Oh, I'm sure it does. The simpler on the surface the music is, the more difficult it is to find the inner truth of it. I don't mean that it should be twisted or distorted, or that a truth should be imposed upon it. That's exactly wrong.

And there is this long line.

It's not only the long line. It is having that incredible faith, the same faith that the composer had in the beauty of simplicity, and out of that faith being able to refashion this piece, to recreate this music in the same spirit of nobility and depth out of which it was written. Dimitri had lost interest in that aspect of it. He liked complexity, and surface complexity toward the end.

In any case, this is just to prepare you. I don't like to say, as so many incoming presidents of organizations tend to say, 'Well, I found this company in dreadful shape and now. . . .' It is so easy to be boastful. Dimitri Mitropoulos was perhaps the greatest genius I have ever known in music. He had, like all of us, faults. Among his faults was this attitude towards orchestral playing itself, this lack of interest in the polish and refinement of playing, in the variety of sounds that one can get from an orchestra. As a result, when I came in we shared the first year. We were associate conductors of the Philharmonic. And then he left. I had it all to myself. And I remember during that first year listening to his performances and observing this very thing, a raggedness, a lack of ensemble, of precision, of intonation. He'd never asked for these things, you see. As long as he had his dynamics he was happy. So I was left with an orchestra that not only was playing roughly, imprecisely, out of tune, and carelessly, but one which was not schooled in playing Haydn, Handel, Bach, Mozart, Vivaldi; and also an orchestra whose morale was very low, because as a result of this deterioration of simple performing standard the orchestra's reputation had kind of gone down.

I hate to say all these things, because it sounds as though I'm denigrating Mitropoulos, whom I worshipped. I'm just trying to say what I think is the truth. I cannot tell you the love I bear and bore Mitropoulos, and I would not say a hurtful word about him for the world. I don't think this is hurtful, because I'm simply trying to describe what is true about this man who was so extraordinary, whose capacities were so enormous for study and comprehension of difficult music, that toward the end of his life he did lose interest in what he considered more simple music. Therefore, when I say the morale of the orchestra was low, I mean that their criticism was very bad at that time in the press. The audiences had dwindled so that an average Sunday afternoon concert was sparsely peopled in Carnegie Hall. It used to be

Sir Adrian Boult

Otto Klemperer

Leonard Bernstein

Ernest Ansermet

Left and above: Leopold Stokowski

Bruno Walter

very depressing to go to a concert in Carnegie Hall on Sunday afternoon. And the orchestra felt this. They didn't feel they played well,
they weren't proud of themselves, they knew they weren't getting large
audiences.

*The players in the New York Philharmonic have got the reputation for being a
pretty tough lot. Has that been your experience?*

No. They seemed so, I must say, at that time, but I think part of it
was this morale business. In the decade since then I think all that has
changed. We give infinitely more concerts than were given then and
it's very hard to find a seat in any of them. The orchestra plays mag-
nificently in tune and with enormous variety.

I think the thing I'm proudest of having achieved with the Philharmonic in this decade is not to have developed a Philharmonic sound.
You know most major orchestras boast of their sound: the Philadelphia
sound, the Boston sound; in fact, some conductors go so far as to name
that sound after their very own names. I find that anti-musical,
dangerous and against the grain of what the intentions and purpose of
an orchestra should be. The purpose of an orchestra is to transmit as
accurately as possible, as movingly as possible, the intention of the
composer that it is performing. If an orchestra has its own sound in
every piece that it plays, it cannot have the sound of the composer.

What I am terribly proud of in the Philharmonic is that it doesn't
have a sound of any sort of its own and that it can change from piece to
piece on a dime, instantaneously, from one sound to another. In this
sense, I feel it is a highly sophisticated orchestra. Maybe having sat
there and listened to so many of my scripts and TV shows and talks,
maybe that has been a sophisticating factor. But whatever it is, I've
certainly tried to develop this non-Philharmonic sound, to develop the
sound that is necessary in moving from Beethoven to Ravel, from
Mozart to Stravinsky to Berg, whatever it is that we're playing.

*Do you think it's possible for a conductor to embrace all fields of the repertoire
with equal success?*

I don't know if it's possible, but it must be the ideal and goal of every
conductor. It is not for me to say whether I can or whether anybody
can. All one can do is hold that up before one as a shining goal. That is
certainly what I've tried to do. We play Haydn symphonies now. Just
this last year we have been doing the 'Paris' set and recording them.

When I listen to those playbacks of the records, I am as proud of those six Haydn symphonies as I can be, because the sound of them is a Haydn sound. It is not a Philharmonic sound, and it's not any orchestra that you can identify. It is the sound of Haydn. Then when I hear the Sibelius symphonies I'm equally proud, because it is a Sibelius sound. I mean, what comes out when we play Sibelius is something fat and solemn and mysterious—and tentative sometimes—and what comes out of the Haydn records is something bright and intimate and intensely cheerful. You couldn't believe it is the same men playing both works. And then we play Mahler, of course.

You identify very strongly with Mahler. I wondered if you had particular difficulties in conducting him.

The only difficulty in conducting Mahler is durability, the ability to last, a simple physical problem of maintaining the intensity, concentration and physical energy that is required. By physical energy, of course, I mean emotional energy too, tension, nervous energy, which is required to take a large Mahler piece from beginning to end. That's the only problem that I have ever found with Mahler, because I find everything so explicit and clear in those scores, so specifically detailed, so copiously annotated, in some cases overly so—footnotes and thousands of signs and accents and inner diminuendi and crescendi. I don't think there is any way of missing Mahler's intention if you have a basic sympathy with the music.

There is this parallel: Mahler composed and conducted; he was a very possessed man; he was pursued by a demon, forever striving. Have you ever analysed why it is that Mahler's music has such a great appeal to you?

You are implying that there is an analogue between us. Well, there are some. Of course, there is being torn between performing and creating, which is a very big split and does tend to create a schizophrenic effect. While they go together very naturally for Mahler and for me, and for Mendelssohn and Beethoven, Berlioz and Wagner, they are still extraordinarily different psychologically as activities, since one activity is a highly public one, the other a highly solitary one. And for it you need a tremendous amount of time, so tremendous an amount of time that time must seem to stop for you while you are composing. You mustn't feel that you must stop at six, because then the real time of music, which in this case I call real, has to take over; and if the clock time is paramount, then you—at least I—can't compose. If your head is full of Mahler and Beethoven it is very hard sometimes to find your own notes. I need time simply to get rid of all the other music that's buzzing around in my head, the Verdi Requiem and Haydn symphonies and Webern, whatever it happens to be.

Do you ever worry that in the end you might feel that you could have achieved more if you had just conducted or more if you had just been a composer?

No, because that is an inconceivable state of being. I can't think of myself as existing just as a composer, or just as a performer, because there are these two sides to my nature. I'm cursed with them, if you wish; call it not a blessing, call it a drawback. The truth of it is I have a side that likes to withdraw and be alone for long continuous periods, and I have a side that wants to be with people, a gregarious side, and that wants to share everything with people. I think that's a key word in everything I do, 'share'. I love to teach so much and I love to make these television programmes, both for young people and for adults, because the minute I know something, or recognize something, or enjoy something, that very second I have to share it. I can't bear keeping it to myself. This is true, strangely enough, even when I write music. If I happen to write something suddenly that I know is good, that's a real *trouvaille*, I can't wait to run to my wife, or child, or friend, or whoever is around, to play it to them. I can't keep it to myself. I think that conducting is born from that—in me, anyway—from that impulse to share what I feel, the excitement, the enthusiasm, the mystery, whatever insights I have about all music with as many people as possible.

May I ask a rather difficult question? It deals with this matter of critical acceptance. There tends to be an attitude towards the conductor of the New York Philharmonic—whoever he may be—on the part of East Coast critics, which has been summed up as, 'Show me, I dare you.' Does criticism impinge on you very much?

Oh yes, I would be lying in my throat if I said anything different. I have been sensitive to criticism: I have been hurt by it, and I have been overjoyed by it, and I have been bored by it, and I have been incensed, but mostly not embittered. None of this has lasted, you see. It is all ephemeral, luckily. Mostly I'm frustrated by it because even the good reviews I get are good for the wrong reasons. There seems to be so little perception among the critics about what really happens. They don't really seem to 'hear', most of them. That is frustrating. I'll tell you what's frustrating about it. You can decide that these critics cannot hear anyway, therefore why read them? Then you are all right. There is no frustration involved. But if you still have enough of the child in you (I suppose it's the child, I don't know what else it is) to make you read your reviews, because of the sheer childish delight of seeing your name in the paper or wanting to know what people are saying about you—I suppose these are all childish impulses, but they're human ones and I still have enough of that, so that I still do read my reviews—then it is frustrating.

I was told that when you were in London recently the only time you got mad was when the critics spent more time discussing your physical gestures than the resulting music.

Now that just drives me crazy. I have read hundreds and hundreds of paragraphs in my life of my so-called choreography. It makes me ill to talk about it. But since I don't prepare my gestures or actions on the podium, I have no idea what I do. I can't really be responsible for them; and that's bad. I am not using this in my defence at all. It would be better if I could make more preparation or think about what I'm going to do on the podium and be less likely to do things that are offensive or distracting from the music. That is what I do agree with. It is very distracting to be visually occupied when you should be aurally occupied. I have no desire to occupy anybody visually. But I simply go about trying to evoke this music from the orchestra in the best way I can and to do what I need to in order to have them play in the way they should play. I don't know what that way is, and the only way I would have of knowing is watching myself on television, which I have had occasion to do many times. But I can't look. Most of the time I have to avert my face. I can't watch myself at all. Sometimes I am in sympathy with people who protest against my podium activities. I think, well, they're justified also in not being able to bear looking. I am very apologetic about it if I am distracting, because I wouldn't do that for the world to any piece of music. But I'm afraid that there's no help for it. I have to do whatever I have to do, and God knows what that is; I don't know. But apparently enough people are not offended by it so that I am still conducting in public.

New York, April 1967

Ernest Ansermet

ROBERT CHESTERMAN: *Mr Ansermet, may I begin in a biographical sense and ask, first of all, if your parents were at all musical?*

ERNEST ANSERMET: Oh yes, my mother was singing and I was playing piano, because she came from a family of peasants who were living in the north of the Canton de Vaud, on the Jura. The whole family of these peasants were all musicians. My great-grandfather had seven sons and each one played two instruments, one wood instrument and one string instrument. I learned myself the clarinet with my uncle and the piano with my mother, and the violin with a violin of my great-grandfather; also, my father had a wonderful bass voice. So I was born in the music, and I must tell you I am always a little shocked when I see so many critics write: Mr Ansermet was a mathematician who then later became a musician. It is quite wrong! I was a musician from my childhood. I was first a musician.

But the question is this: first of all I was rather lazy about technical questions. When I was playing the piano or violin, instead of working on the technique, I invented melodies, and so I could not make a career as a pianist or a violinist. And in our country at that time it was impossible to live from music, even if I would have been a good composer. So I had to choose another way to make a living and I chose the way of mathematics master.

You grew up in Switzerland, here in Suisse Romande country, didn't you?

Oh yes, in Vevey.

Is it true that the people who come from Suisse Romande are very painstaking, patient, rather conservative people?

No, they have much temperament. There is a very great difference between the Canton de Vaud and Geneva. In Geneva they are intellectual people, critical people; but in my country, Vaud, they are all peasants. So they have much temperament and they are also very free in their meaning, and I think that is what gives us more vitality than the people of Geneva.

When did you actually turn to conducting as such in a professional sense?

Well, during my university days beside mathematics I was always practising music, studying harmony, counterpoint, and all that is important in music. I knew by memory the score of a symphony by Beethoven when I was already a student. And so I was ready. I had little hope in my composing, but I had great aspiration to conduct, always. But I didn't believe it would be possible.

But when I was teaching in the college of Lausanne, the pupils of this college formed an orchestra that I had to conduct. Then I had the chance to go to Germany to observe the great conductors, and that is the time in Berlin when I saw Mottl and Nikisch.

Is it possible for you to summarize what you feel about conducting as an art?

Yes, I think I have on this point rather old ideas.

You know, for me conducting is not a profession. The profession for me is to be a musician first of all. And if the musician can conduct, then it is a function and he is called to conduct. For instance, a man cannot decide to become a general or to become a statesman, but he can decide to become a soldier or to become a politician. Depending on his chances and merits, then he will be called one day to be a general, or a statesman. So it was in the old time.

For us, conducting came not from teaching. We didn't learn conducting in my generation in the classroom but in the workshop, in the workshop of practical music. All the conductors of or about my generation, Furtwängler, Klemperer, Kleiber, and others, did not have lessons in conducting. But we had models. For instance, the young conductors who were devoted to opera worked in an opera house as an assistant conductor, as an accompanist of the choir, as a soloist, and then they were formed. This kind of quite practical formation was possible because at that time all the music was in three or four and the technique of conducting three bars or four bars is very easy; in one hour you know everything. So the question of technical conducting was not a problem for us. Of course, when we had seen how our models, Nikisch or Mottl or others, were conducting, the question was if we had the freedom of gesture for doing it. That was the whole question. I have a good friend here in Geneva who is a great composer and he wanted to conduct, but he was unable to make a gesture of the arm without making at the same time a gesture with the body. So the players did not know which was the good gesture: the gesture of the body or the gesture of the arm which followed!

The Italians are very often good conductors because they speak with the hands. They have these expressive gestures which is the fact of conducting. But came Stravinsky, and instead of having bars in three or four he had these irregular bars, unequal cadences—five-sixteenths, three-sixteenths, two-sixteenths—and a constant change of bars. Then the technique was more complicated and more subtle.

I began my career just at this moment. I was the first to introduce these Stravinsky rhythms in Paris, in London, in Berlin—where I conducted the first German performance of *The Rite of Spring* in 1922— and I had to invent this new technique. And as it was rather difficult then the young conductors began to ask for lessons, and this method of teaching conducting in lessons directed the attention of the conductor on the technique, not on the music! Then came a second element, especially in North America, where the conductors had to perform before a public which was not educated in music, and they had a certain role to play in order to convince. And they became showmen, giving more importance to the gesture they were giving to the public than to the gesture they were giving to the players. For my part, I think I can say I have never made a gesture which was not necessary for the players; I have never played to the public. The public could receive the music, and I hope understand it, but the question was the players.

Could you say what is the most difficult thing for a conductor to convey to his players?

The conductor cannot explain to the players how they have to play, because they know their instruments better than the conductor. But he has to indicate to them what they cannot know: the phrasing, the right accent, the right tempo, and the right sonorous value they are to give to their notes, because there are voices in the orchestra which remain in the shadow and other voices which have to be put in the light. That is the task of the conductor.

Out of these various points you mention, would you say the most difficult thing of all, perhaps, to convey properly to an orchestra is that of rhythm?

Yes. The whole question is that the conductor must understand that the musical time is not a metric time. That is contrary to what is taught in many schools, because they see always the written beat; but every beat is already a cadence. The beat is only marked by a crotchet or a dotted crotchet. In the first case the crotchet is the value of two quavers. In the second the dotted crotchet has the value of three quavers, and so it is already a cadence. So the single beat of the conductor indicates the cadence, and that is the first question. The conductor doesn't beat the time, he beats the cadence. That is the point.

Now, the tempo has to be felt. It is not a matter of metronome, it is a matter of musical feeling. The musical feeling develops in a certain tempo and this tempo is indicated by the conductor, or by his gesture—by this cadence.

When you conduct, do you always conduct with a score?

Yes, generally. I think it is impossible to conduct really a work without knowing by memory, by heart, the score, because you can only conduct a score well if you know the music perfectly, and so you must have studied it and you know how it is made. You know the form, you know in each moment where you are going and when it will stop, and so on, and how it is phrased. But I am against conducting by memory, because it leads one to conduct the principal melodic line and to forget the secondary voices.

When you were talking earlier, you touched on conductors whom you had seen as a young man. You mentioned Nikisch and you mentioned Mottl. Could you tell me what it was about Nikisch that particularly struck you?

Nikisch was a great virtuoso of the orchestra. He was profoundly a musician. That is why his conducting was so efficient. But he had a manner of conducting which is not ours today. He was conducting always before the time. You see, he had no up-beat; he gave the beat and the musicians followed. That is the first example of what happened later with Furtwängler, who gave the beat and the moment after came the playing. It was very difficult for a conductor like myself to conduct the Philharmonic in Berlin because they had this habit.

Sir Adrian Boult says that with Nikisch it was all in the stick, that the stick conveyed everything. Would you agree?

Well, the whole arm I would say, not only the stick.

Now Mottl was more *pratique*, less virtuoso, more precise. But I have an example of Weingartner. For me that was a classical example. I also had some lessons from Weingartner in order to make precise my ideas about how to give the beat, and so on. And then I had my master Francisco de Lacerda, who was an excellent conductor. He was my model. He was a Portuguese and he was an assistant of d'Indy in Paris. He came to conduct in Montreux and that is where I could observe him. When he left Montreux I was his successor.

Was it in his gesture that he was so extraordinary?

Fantastique! He had small arms, short arms, and so his gesture was extremely precise and extremely energetic.

Would you say his gesture was more precise than that of Nikisch?

The gesture of Nikisch was more decorative.

Stravinsky once made rather a malicious comment about Nikisch. He said that Nikisch tended to plan programmes for the betterment of himself, not with the music to the fore.

No, it is not quite right. Of course, he cultivated the music from his time and his taste. For example, he was the man who introduced Tchaikovsky in Germany; but he was also the greater interpreter of Beethoven and all the Classics.

Coming back to Weingartner—he really started the reaction, didn't he, against this Romantic kind of conducting?

Yes, against the kind of Romantic conducting which emphasized the sentimentality of the music. Weingartner had a more Classical feeling, more rigorous in the form.

This particularly attracted you?

Yes, and it has remained in my conducting.

It is an intellectual thing really?

It is not quite an intellectual thing. It is a question of taste and also of feeling. You know, many critics feel that the conductor gives feeling in the music only when the conductor's feeling is emphasized: extensive and exaggerated, for instance, in a crescendo, diminuendo, rallentando.

But the feeling is everywhere in music. You do not need to exaggerate. If you play the music right, there is always feeling.

When did you first meet Toscanini?

In 1930, in Berlin. I was there with the Russian Ballet for the first musical festival of Berlin, and Toscanini was with La Scala. We met. And again, later, in Lucerne—he was called to initiate the musical weeks of Lucerne during the summer. The first concert was conducted by Toscanini in Triebschen, the house of Wagner, where he conducted the *Siegfried Idyll* in the same orchestral disposition that Richter had done before. The same day we had an orchestral concert where I had to conduct a Haydn symphony and *La Valse* of Ravel. Toscanini was so satisfied with my *Valse* that he told me, 'You must conduct that in America.' And after the last war he called me to the NBC to conduct a concert during his holidays, and then I conducted *La Valse*.

How did you find the NBC orchestra at that time?

Fantastic; the best orchestra I have ever conducted. Well, since then we had a master orchestra in London, the Philharmonia, which was formed by Walter Legge. I don't yet know the New Philharmonia. I will conduct this New Philharmonia in November when I have to re-record the *Firebird* ballet in the original scoring. This ballet is extremely difficult to play for the orchestra. The writing of Stravinsky is very complicated, very subtle. I think you must have a first-rate orchestra for playing it. That is why I asked to make this record for Decca with the New Philharmonia.

To come back, if I may, to Toscanini. Were you unreservedly an admirer?

Well, I adored Toscanini as a person and he was so purely a musician. He would think only of the music. Now I could not agree always with his tempi. They were on the fast side because he believed in the written music. I mean he would be true to what is written, always. What is written indicates something, but it is not the real thing; it is something different, you know. I will give you an example. I had made a record of the *Prague* Symphony. He heard the record and at the *Andante* he said, 'Much too slow.' I told him, 'But how? That is an Andante.' 'No, it is a dance,' he said. So I could not agree. But I understood that for him it was so. He played what he felt. But, of course, he was marvellous in a lot of musical works. For instance, all the Italian opera.

When somebody has heard Toscanini conducting Verdi or Puccini, he has heard the ideal.

He was very objective, wasn't he?

Very objective, very objective. I can give you another example. I had to conduct his NBC orchestra in the First Suite of Bach, with the Aria. In this Aria comes a moment when we usually make an appoggiatura. But the appoggiatura is not written by Bach. So when I made an appoggiatura, he told me, 'I don't make this appoggiatura; it is not written.' I could not immediately answer. But I went to the library in New York and got the book of Quantz, the flute player who has written how the music of Bach should be played. He wrote this: 'It is not only necessary to make an appoggiatura when it is written, but also when good taste indicates it; and, for instance, if all the voices come on a perfect harmony, it is good to postpone this harmony by an appoggiatura from the high or the low note.' I brought this text to Toscanini. I told him that was why I made the appoggiatura. He told me, 'Too difficult for me.' He was a simple man!

I read that he planned everything very carefully in his rehearsals so that there really wasn't much room for error in a performance.

Oh yes, it was all fixed. When he had rehearsed it was fixed, and the performance was exactly the same as the last rehearsal.

I want to ask you how you approach your rehearsals?

It is about the same. My point is not the exact technical playing. It is the exact expression of the music. I try to reach this level of expression in my rehearsal and then it is ready for the performance.

I would just like to touch on the subject of younger conductors. Do you have many opportunities to hear any of them?

I have heard Bernstein and Maazel.

Could I ask you for your impressions?

I appreciate immensely Bernstein. I think he is a very great musical talent. But it is a question of attitude. He has taken this attitude of showman. I saw him when he was conducting the Passion of Bach. He was really making the mimic of Jesus on the Cross. He was suffering like Jesus. So we had two messages: the message of the music, which was expressing the suffering of Jesus, and the message of the mimic of Bernstein. I did not know if I should see, or hear. I hope he will understand one day that this is absolutely unuseful.

With Maazel the question is no more the question of showmanship. The question then is technical approach to the music. His attention is directed towards the exactitude of this quaver, this crotchet, this pause, and so on.

We were talking about objective playing. Pierre Boulez made the comment that scores must now be interpreted in the spirit of the time.

It is quite wrong! They should be interpreted in the spirit of the composer! That is, of the time of the composer, of course. It is quite wrong. It is exactly the same as Stravinsky. Stravinsky believed in the exactitude of the metronome mark. Two years ago I was in Hamburg conducting at the Opera, where the Intendant is Liebermann. Liebermann came from Los Angeles, where he had visited Stravinsky in order to ask him questions about *The Rake's Progress*, and he told me that Stravinsky had said to him, 'Tell your conductor not to observe too much my metronome marks, because after all he must find for himself the right movement.' So, arrived at eighty-four years of age, Stravinsky was changing his mind!

Mr Ansermet, people think of you so much for the first performances that you gave in this incredible period—the Stravinsky works, Prokofiev, Manuel de Falla's Three-Cornered Hat—*and yet I think they tend to overlook the fact that you have a vast repertoire. Do you ever feel that your attention to the Classics is overlooked?*

Well, the point is this. At that time when I was beginning to conduct it was in very important situations with Diaghilev and the Russian Ballet. We performed *The Rite of Spring* for the first time after the war; before, it was only conducted once by Monteux, that's all. And then there was *Apollon Musagète, Les Noces, Renard,* and so on. I was so absorbed by this new task of conducting that I could not at the same time be devoted to the Classics. I have never neglected the Classics, but I had to employ my forces for this new music, the music of Stravinsky, Prokofiev, Ravel, Debussy, and then Hindemith and Bartók. But, of course, the day came when this was completed. I had resolved the problems. I knew how to do them, and so I could come back and bring to maturity my feelings about the Classics. That is why I have given so much importance in the last ten or twenty years to my interpretation of the Classics.

Turning to this matter of repertoire, I wonder if the Classical repertoire makes the greatest demands upon a conductor?

The greatest demand in the matter of interpretation, but not in the matter of technique. Of course, modern works make a great demand in technical matters: the rhythm and harmony are more complicated, the tempo is more often changing, and so on. In Classical music we have an equal tempo, the polyphony is not too complicated, the chords are simple. But then the whole point is the interpretation, the feeling—the musical feeling.

As one gets older, does one have to confine one's repertoire more? Schnabel, in his biography, said that in his last years he had to live what he termed the intensive life—that he would only play Beethoven sonatas, Schubert piano works, and some Mozart. Do you find that you have to confine yourself?

No, I do not. But I think I am more able to do these works today because I have acquired this maturity and so I have a special interest in playing Classical music.

You conduct Haydn a lot, don't you?

Oh yes, very much. We are coming back to Haydn. I spoke very often with Furtwängler about that. He told me, 'You know, to my mind, Haydn is more of a symphonic composer than Mozart. The sense of symphony is to be found in Haydn.' That is also my point of view today. That is why, as the 'London' symphonies by Haydn were all recorded by Sir Thomas Beecham, I recorded the 'Paris' symphonies which came before and are absolutely marvellous.

Interpretatively, they are not as difficult though, are they, as, say, the last three great Mozart symphonies?

Well, it is another kind of difficulty. The last Mozart symphonies depend very much on the right feeling of the C major, G minor, E flat. With the Haydn symphonies, the spirit of the symphony has to be found in them and to be realized by the interpretation.

We were talking just a moment ago about this great period when all these ballets were being performed. I read that Pierre Monteux, who also was conducting a lot of ballets at this time—as he conducted the first performance of The Rite of

Spring—*made the comment that he had never thought of himself as becoming a ballet conductor.*

It was just an opportunity? Oh yes, it is true.

How did you feel yourself about conducting ballet?

Well, I was rather more inclined to the ballet than Monteux, because Monteux was a *quartettiste*. He was playing Classical quartets and he was a viola soloist in Paris. But I was always attracted by music where the rhythm has a special importance. That is why, for instance, I was conducting very much Russian music, but the Russian music of the North—Rimsky-Korsakov, Borodin. And that is why I became a friend of Stravinsky, because Stravinsky came to my concert in Montreux and heard me playing Rimsky, and he told me, 'Well, I see that.' And many Russians have told me, even when I was in Russia, that I had the sense of Russian music on the rhythmical side.

To come back to The Rite of Spring. *Do I understand that Pierre Monteux conducted a concert version after the première in 1913 and then Stravinsky revised the work?*

Monteux conducted this concert version and then I proposed to Stravinsky to revise the final dance, because he had written the final dance in bars like five-sixteenths and if it is not clearly indicated the conductor doesn't know what to do. So I suggested to Stravinsky to make a new reduction by dividing these bars into their exact components. I still have my sketch. I sent it to Stravinsky. He approved and a new print was made.

After the First World War, perhaps in 1920, one day I got a cable from Diaghilev in Paris: 'I am preparing *The Rite of Spring* with choreography by Massine aux Champs-Elysées—do come and conduct.' I went immediately to Paris. I was ready, I knew the work very well, and we did this *reprise* of *The Rite of Spring*. Then we played it in London, and then I had to play it in many concerts, especially in Berlin. This was the first performance in Germany, in 1922.

When you did that performance at the Champs-Elysées, people must have gone bearing in mind what had happened in 1913. Were you aware of any feeling of tension in the audience when you conducted?

In these first years there was still a certain tension, but far away from the tension of 1913. First of all, because I think the work was better than the choreography of Nijinsky; better also because the hearers had already absorbed the new turn of music, the new harmonies.

I think that with many people it is the rather impersonal, detached quality of Stravinsky's music that they find hard to come to terms with.

Well, it is always hard in the beginning. But with more knowledge of the music you accept it, you know. For me, the only question with Stravinsky was this: his music is excellent, but in the way he will do it —I mean make it—his music is not the same thing as the music of other composers before him. For the Romantic and for the Classical composers, it was always an expression of their own feelings. For Debussy, it was also the impression of the expression of his own feelings about nature, and so on. But with Stravinsky, no. It is a representative, a figurative music. It is an application. And this application of the music to such pictorial effects or representative intention is wonderfully realized.

But we must state that there is not the same human value as in music which is the expression of the man. That is the point on which we disagree. I admire immensely all that he does. It is always perfect, his technique, his writing, and his conception. But I don't like his aesthetic. And the aesthetic was always our point of discussion. It is the point where we disagreed, completely. That is why he was very angry with me after these discussions. But some years ago we have made again friendship.

There came a proposition from New York asking me to conduct one of the concerts in the Stravinsky Festival at the Lincoln Center. It was two years ago, and first I said I could not go because I had something else to do. But they insisted, telling me it was the wish of Stravinsky that I conduct this concert of *Perséphone*. So I said, 'If it is the wish of Stravinsky, I will come.' And I went. Unfortunately, Stravinsky was ill and could not come to New York, but I wrote him a letter telling him about the concert and telling him how satisfied I was to have conducted. Then he wrote to me saying how our disagreement was very painful for him until now, but with my letter he was quite cured.

Discussions of style and form crop up frequently with Stravinsky's music and I know you have written very vividly on orchestral style, so may I ask you the question: what is style?

I mean by orchestral style the way players approach the music. If a conductor comes to an orchestra as a guest conductor, he has no time to train the orchestra or to educate the orchestra. He has just to beat as he can and to obtain from the orchestra what he can obtain. But if somebody is a regular conductor, as I was with my orchestra in Geneva, he has to educate the orchestra. You can educate it in different ways. You can look for the external effect, for the technical perfection, for the brilliance of the sonority, and so on. Or you can look for the right phrasing, the right accentuation, the right tempo and the right sonorous value of every voice. That is style. The manner you approach the orchestra, so you approach the music.

There are several kinds of orchestras. There are orchestras trained for being brilliant, technically brilliant, and others which are trained for giving more the truth of the music, the expression of the music. There are other orchestras, namely in Germany, which are trained for giving always—as in Vienna—sentimentality. Every phrase is sentimental, is expressive in this sense. But I don't like sentimentality in all music. If, for instance, I have to play a work by Debussy in Vienna with the Vienna Philharmonic, which is a first-rate orchestra, I have great difficulty. I was never able to obtain a perfect performance of the *Firebird* Suite—the Suite of 1919—with the Vienna Philharmonic, because they had not the equality of sound and the exactitude of rhythm that is required for this music.

So the style is different. The style of the Vienna orchestra is not the same as the Berlin Philharmonic, not the same as the Philharmonia in London, not the same as the Orchestre de Paris, and so on.

I tried to give this style to my orchestra here, and this style was the right expression, the right phrasing, not the effect but the inner truth of the music. Of course, this applies to every composer. So we try to give Beethoven the right spirit of Beethoven, or give Haydn the right spirit, and so on. If you have another kind of conductor, you will hear a symphony by Haydn and all the notes will be perfectly well done, but Haydn will be absent. The question is to feel Haydn through the symphony, or to feel Beethoven or to feel Mozart or Debussy. I have often heard *Nuages* or *Fêtes* of Debussy as if it would be *The Ride of the Valkyries*. But it is not the same!

Can you recall your first meeting with Debussy?

Oh yes. You know, I had two friends who were close friends of Debussy, Robert Godet and my master Francisco de Lacerda. The first time they introduced me to him was in a concert in Paris in 1910 where he was conducting the first performance of *Rondes de Printemps*. And after the concert I went to him and we met in the artists' room and spoke a little, and I could observe him with all the people who were there.

But then in 1917, when I gave the first performance of *Parade* by Erik Satie in Paris, with the Russian Ballet, he was there and he invited me for the following afternoon. So I had a full afternoon with him in his home on the Bois de Boulogne and, of course, then I had a better acquaintance. We discussed many of the tempi of his works and musical questions of the day and so on. For instance, I was asking him some question about the *Nocturnes*. He took his score of the *Nocturnes* and I saw it was full of corrections with pencils of all colours—red pencil, blue pencil, green pencil. I said, 'What is right?' He told me, 'I don't know. Take the score with you and bring it back in a few days and say what seems good to you.' So I have made for myself a score of these *Nocturnes*. That is why if you hear, for instance, my recording of them you will see that the Sirènes don't sing what they sing in the other recordings.

He was a man very reserved, you know, an aristocratic nature. I had the impression always that he was apart from his surroundings. He had few friendships. His only friendship was with the old Godet, who was a friend since they were young, and Lacerda who came after. He was very friendly with Satie and every week he took lunch with him. But he had his opinion about Satie. He was not taking him for a great musician but for a charming and an interesting man. I had the impression he was very alone, very *solitaire*.

He was rather short, wasn't he, in appearance? He wasn't a tall man.

Oh, he was about my height. No, he was not very short. When he became older he was a little thicker than when he was young. But not very much.

Very Bohemian in appearance?

No, no, not at all! Very elegant. When I saw him for the first time in a rehearsal he had a *chapeau melon*, the hat of the London people. He was Bohemian when he was young; then he had a hat like the *artiste*, and the necktie also. But later, no more—especially since he was the husband of Mme Bardac.

It is interesting reading biographies of these famous figures of the past. One thing that I recall is that it was said that Debussy was always short of money.

Yes, yes. He had always sorrows because, before his second marriage, he was very poor; and after he had to pay a pension to his first wife. So it was rather difficult.

Do you think this shortage of money was, in a way, an inspiration to him?

No, not at all. I think it is never an influence on the writing of the musician. When the musician makes music he is outside of his practical life and the practical life is no influence on him—unless he is a bad musician!

There are very contradictory accounts that one reads about Debussy's character: that he was shy yet outspoken, that he was a very independent man but an envious man.

Oh no, he was not envious at all. He was convinced of himself. He had his way of seeing things, and he would not be disturbed by others. But, of course, he could not be in harmony with people who were all interested in the political or economic life. He was just for his music.

Did he have a sharp sense of humour?

Oh yes, very sharp. And you can see it not only in his music—in some of the Preludes, for instance—but also in his writings.

The best book on Debussy is by Dietschy. It is an excellent book and gives really all details. It is published by the same publisher as my book, la Baconnière de Neuchâtel.

Do you know the two volumes by Edward Lockspeiser?

Yes, but Lockspeiser is a man who is looking for details and who exaggerates on many points.

You mentioned that Debussy spoke of Satie. Did he mention Stravinsky at all?

Oh yes. At the time when Stravinsky gave *Firebird* and *Petrushka* in Paris he was very enthusiastic about Stravinsky. But already he was not so enthusiastic about his music as about his scoring. He said, 'He's fantastic for the scoring.' And you find these expressions in the book published by Robert Godet, with the letters of Debussy. So he was enthusiastic about *Petrushka*. But when he heard *The Rite of Spring* he already had some doubt. He told me, 'He is like a German who during the war would make a beefsteak with wood.' Stravinsky believed that one could make music with rhythm. It was real for the Negroes, but not for us. And so he was already in doubt.

He played a duo-piano performance of the Rite *with Stravinsky.*

Oh yes, and I heard it. I can show you the photograph here of Debussy and Stravinsky together in the home of Debussy. He was giving a testimony of his friendship and his admiration for Stravinsky at that time. And he remained so, but with critical sense; of course, he was not an adulator. But Stravinsky has interpreted that very badly in his last books: he says Debussy was a wrong man, a liar, and so on. It is quite wrong. All that Stravinsky said in his last book with Robert Craft is terrible.

You did not do any first performances of Debussy's work, did you?

No, no. But he knew from Godet that I was playing much of his music. I was conducting his works in Paris, after his death, and Mrs Debussy was there and told me how they appreciated this.

Were you living permanently in Paris at this time?

One year, 1928. I was conductor with Forestier with the OSP—Orchestre Symphonique de Paris.

You weren't present at the first performance of Pelléas et Mélisande, *then?*

No. That was given in 1902. I went the following year to a Saturday afternoon performance. But it was still with the same singers and the same conductor, Messager. And I was at that time teaching mathematics in Lausanne.

There was an enormous division at this time, wasn't there, between admirers and detractors of the opera?

Oh yes, that was a real struggle. It was what we call a *coup monté*, a kind of organization against *Pelléas*.

Generally, though, with many people it's still unpopular even now. They don't seem to grasp the idiom.

I don't know. I think today people are tired not of *Pelléas*, but of Maeterlinck. They find the music attractive, but Maeterlinck boring. But I don't think so. I think the Maeterlinck words are so exactly the words for this music that I accept them, without judging them from the pure literary point of view.

Your last recording, which was very well reviewed by many, many people, is really your final statement on Pelléas?

I would do it again.

What sort of influence was Wagner, would you say, on Pelléas?

The harmony of Debussy has been influenced by the harmony of Wagner, especially *Tristan* and *Parsifal*.

The influence of Wagner was incredibly strong in Paris in those days, wasn't it?

Much less on Debussy than on others. D'Indy or Dukas were more influenced by Wagner than Debussy. Wagner was a revelation for Debussy, but then from that he took what he would take and made his own harmony, which is quite different. The melodic side was more in the light. The melody is quite independent of the harmony, it develops itself on any harmony. For instance, take the *Prélude à l'Après-Midi d'un Faune*. You have the air of the flute and this melody, after being played alone, comes on a D major chord and it is in E major; and it comes later always on new harmonies, remaining the same. So the melody of Debussy is independent in a certain way from the harmony which accompanies it. And in this melodic line of Debussy, with many, many works, you observe the pentatonic scale. Debussy chose it because it is indeterminate tonally. In practising the pentatonic melody, his melody was free and he could put any kind of harmony under the melody.

Mentioning the Prélude à l'Apres-Midi d'un Faune, *at the première there was a great deal of dissension over this work, wasn't there?*

Oh no, not at the première. The première was successful! It was even encored. No, later I attended a performance of *La Mer*, conducted by Debussy, when it was *sifflé*. I was struggling in the hall with somebody who was whistling!

But Nijinsky caused a sensation, didn't he, with the choreography for the Prélude *which he did with Diaghilev?*

Ah, but Diaghilev was quite unsatisfied with this choreography from Nijinsky. He was not satisfied at all! Because, for Debussy, the faun was

was fond of Turner, he was fond of Degas, he was fond of many
ers, of course. But these paintings had no influence.

ink that a lot of this also comes out when in La Mer *there is this Hokusai*
on the title page.

was the time the Japanese were discovered in Paris.

es this not tend to confuse people, indicating that there is a link between
ng and the music?

ey are parallel, but the one is not making the other.

at makes for me the greatness of Debussy? He is great in the same
that Beethoven is great, Mozart is great, Schubert is great,
se all these musicians, through their music, give us a certain vision
world. There is a Beethoven world, a certain manner of being in
orld: the pathetic and human world of Beethoven, the *galant*
of Mozart, the landscape of Schubert. Debussy gives you also a
vision of the world. The world of Debussy is a world where
and all things have a soul. For him the waves on the ocean, the
ight, all that has a soul. So it is a vision of the world which is
tely Debussyan, communicated to us by the music.

hears comments made of Debussy by Pierre Boulez now. He also said that
ressionist idea of Debussy is wrong, that one shouldn't concentrate on this.
r attitude to Debussy is different, really, from that of Pierre Boulez, is it

yes, because I consider Debussy's work is based on feeling. With
it is based on calculation.

rn composers, though, have tended to look at Debussy and say that he
model for that which followed.

not at all. There is no contact at all, to my mind, between
y and the actual avant-garde. Debussy had no influence even
vinsky. Stravinsky was more influenced by Ravel, and by his
Rimsky-Korsakov. He took something from Debussy, some
tail, but he didn't enter into the spirit of the music of Debussy.
la, who is in the spirit of the music, is a real follower of Debussy.
in certain respects—not in all—because Ravel comes back, to
d, to Saint-Saëns, but with new harmonies and new kinds of

very flexible, and Nijinsky had made a quite me
Debussy was not keen at all on Nijinsky doing
with *Jeux*, when it was commissioned by D
choreography from Nijinsky had not sufficient
a dream of a summer afternoon. With Nijinsky
much in the light.

Was there a danger at this time, in all these ballets
on, of the dance overruling the music?

There was always a tension between the
musician. I can tell you, for instance, when I c
first performance of *The Three-Cornered Hat* by
last dance in the tempo Falla had given to
taking another tempo on the stage, and Di
giving me another tempo, telling me, 'You ar
are too slow.' And I had to find the middle v

May I turn to this matter of the influence on Deb
does seem to be great confusion over this. In one i
High Fidelity Magazine *you said that you*
influenced Debussy.

No, not at all; much more poetry, Mallarm
painting. In his home you could not find an
sionists, not at all. The label 'Impressionist'
wrong. The point is this:
In the Classical time, the music was an
sadness, and so on. With Debussy, he was m
feeling was always a feeling of something wh
the clouds, the water, the moonlight. So yo
of Debussy the thing which moves him—
clouds, the moonlight, and so on. So of co
the feeling of something, are an impression
that Impressionist. Because it is full of harn
the feeling of these impressions. So it is a ly
an Impressionist. He is a lyrical musician.
music is only one exterior aspect of the mu

He was, nevertheless, interested in painting, b
saw pictures by Turner, and he mentioned Turner

What did you think of Debussy as an orchestrator?

Rimsky-Korsakov has made the remark that there are two kinds of musician in regard to scoring: the one makes the score so that if you just play the notes, you have everything; the other makes the score so that it is not sufficient to play the notes, for you must play them in a certain manner, in a certain feeling, in order to get the right sound. Beethoven belongs to this last category, and Debussy too. You can play Ravel exactly as written; it will sound. Not Debussy. With Debussy you must first understand the music, and then arrange your performance in order to realize the musical idea.

Do you think there is a great deal of difference between the orchestration of the early Nocturnes *and the* Images?

Well, in the *Images* it is more complicated. That is all. The *Nocturnes* are very simple, but even the *Nocturnes* must be treated by the conductor in the spirit of Debussy. If not, it may be quite wrong. I have heard performances of *Nuages* and *Fêtes* which were quite wrong. If, for instance, with *Nuages* the conductor will make what we call 'expression', it would be quite wrong. It must be a very quiet line, a pure line, equal. Because the expression is in the line.

Which orchestral work gives you the greatest pleasure now?

La Mer. But I gave also with great pleasure *Rondes de Printemps*. *Rondes de Printemps* is one of the most difficult works I know to interpret. It is terribly difficult. But it is marvellous. One day I had to conduct *Rondes de Printemps* in Paris and Ravel told me, after the concert, 'It was very good. You have done as well as possible with this bad scoring.' But I told him it is not badly scored. It is difficult to realize. That is the point. And now, you know, I have scored myself the *Épigraphes Antiques*, which were written for two pianos, and I have tried to write them in the style of Debussy.

At the end of his life, do you feel that Debussy would have continued with the revolutionary developments that he introduced earlier, or do you feel there was a falling off in his composition?

For me, first of all, his creation was not revolutionary. It was creative. He created a new world of music. He created new harmonies, new ways of writing, a new style. The last sonata gives us an idea of what he would have done after. But, you know, I think in our time a composer cannot indefinitely compose. He comes to the day where he has made what he had to do. Mozart was dead at thirty-five, but he had given us about all that he could give. What could he give more? Another *Don Giovanni*, another *Figaro*? But it would add nothing essential to his works. I think all the composers have a certain limit in their possibility. When Debussy was composing, he was not like these young men you have today, saying, 'I will make something new.' Not at all! He would make something which would be good for him. But not to be new.

Mr Ansermet, would you say that it's very easy to talk about Debussy?

No, it is extremely difficult. And most times when Debussy is discussed the questions are badly exposed. The point, I think, is this: most musicologists have a curious way of looking on the story of music. They think that music has a certain law—a law of tonality, of form and so on—which was fixed in the time of the Classics, by Haydn, Beethoven, Mozart and Bach. And then all who came after were no longer observing all the rules of that time, and so they called these musicians revolutionaries. For being new, you had to be a revolutionary. And being revolutionary, you are new. But it is quite wrong. Because music is a language, and this language is developed through the ages, exactly as the English or the German or the French has developed through the ages, and each new composer after the Classics has found a new form of this language. It was not a revolution. It was creation, just creation.

All the norm of form and scoring and instrumentation was acquired by the end of the nineteenth century, and then it was finished. You could not change. What you could do was only to employ this language in a way which was personal to the composer. That is, to make a new style in this language. That was the situation of Debussy. He was the first composer entirely liberated from the influence of the time. But before Debussy, even when the composers were making novelties, they were writing in the style of their time. He was completely liberated of that. He was not writing in the style of Saint-Saëns or César Franck. That is why he is so free. He is the musician of freedom. Everything is free with him. He has invented new harmonies, a new way of harmonic development, and a new form of melody. He is freedom in person. But then came this young generation of musicians who have, to my mind, not understood Debussy, and believe they must be revolutionary again and they must make something new. No. They must make new music! That is different. . . .

You first formed your orchestra, the Suisse Romande, in 1918, I believe.

Yes, fifty years ago. We will have the fiftieth anniversary at the end of November.

How did you go about forming the orchestra?

It was because in this country we had, at the end of the First World War, no major orchestra. There was only a small orchestra in the Geneva Theatre, but an orchestra for the commonplace French opera—Massenet, Charpentier, and so on. Lausanne had no orchestra, and so I realized that we could have an orchestra only with the agreement of the French-speaking Swiss, that is what we call Suisse Romande. And so we decided to form a special symphony orchestra only for concerts. We were helped by sponsors. Rich people would give their money.

In forming the orchestra I took the woodwind players principally from France, the brass players principally from Vienna, the string players from Belgium and Italy. We did not have sufficient Swiss players at that time. But since then these foreign players have developed pupils who have replaced them in the orchestra, and now we have mostly Swiss players. Of course, the orchestra was not large, about fifty or sixty-odd players who we could engage only for six months. And so my effort was to try to obtain a longer period or to obtain work during the summer, and also to have more players. In 1930, with the great crisis in America, many of our sponsors could no longer give their money, and we tried to obtain more subscribers, but paying a little less. It was good until 1935. In that year the Swiss Radio decided to place its orchestra in Lausanne, not in Geneva. We had no more resources.

So the Société de l'Orchestre de la Suisse Romande was dissolved, and as the players were there, and would not go to Lausanne, they asked me to form a co-operative. We worked in a co-operative with very low salaries for three years. During this time I prepared a plan to be submitted to the Swiss Radio for presenting the orchestra in Geneva. I told the Swiss Radio, 'You have now in Lausanne an orchestra of forty-five players. If you accept my plan I will give you in Geneva an orchestra of eighty-four players for the same price.' After three years of struggle my plan was adopted. It is called here 'The Plan Ansermet'. The orchestra disappeared from Lausanne, came to Geneva, and I

formed the new orchestra of eighty-four players. Since then we have
struggled to obtain more subscriptions from the State or the city in
order to give longer contracts to the orchestra, to have more players.
We are now 120 and all are engaged for the year.

How many of those are Swiss now?

I think three-quarters.

*Do you think that the actual standard of orchestral playing today is very much
higher than it was, say, in 1935?*

Oh yes. The exigency of the public is much higher, and it is a
necessity. It is now difficult to realize, because there is a lack of string
players in the world. The young people have no more time or not
sufficient money to study the violin for seven years before getting a
living. And so it is difficult to find good violinists. But up till now we
could realize that and I hope we will continue to find the necessary
players. It is faster to become a flute player than to become a violinist.

*You were speaking of public awareness. People demand virtuoso orchestras
more now than they did.*

Yes, because the public is less *musicien* than it was. I made this
observation about thirty years ago. There were two kinds of country,
in my view: the country where the people are very musical—and in
this country you can play badly, but it is not disturbing because you
are so musical that you enjoy the music anyhow, if it is badly played or
not; and the country which is not musical, like France, where you must
play perfectly if you want to catch the attention of the public. But now,
everywhere, we ask for good playing.

You feel that the actual appreciation of music, for music's sake, is lacking?

Yes. And for performance. Exactly. I can tell you that I have conducted orchestras in Czechoslovakia, in Poland, in Germany, not in the
big cities but in smaller cities where there were very bad orchestras,
but the public was delighted because they heard music; they were not
looking for the performance. I have often been in concerts in New
York where I observed that the hearers were very superficial. For
instance, once I heard Koussevitzky playing the *Pathétique* and it was
a very good performance and I was very moved. The last note was not
finished and the people around me said, 'Now, where are we going?'
They were already out of the music! I think that somebody who really

appreciates the work needs to remain a little longer in the impressions he has received.

I think that there is another side to this. John Culshaw in his book called Ring Resounding, *based on his experiences recording the* Ring *cycle in Vienna, was discussing this matter about young people and musical appreciation. He said that it was quite wrong to say that people did not have as much musical appreciation now as they did in earlier times, simply because the gramophone had made people far more musically aware. You are saying the contrary?*

No, I don't agree with you at all. Because, to my mind, for being a musician you must practise the music. You must have played an instrument or sing—even badly—but make music. It is in the making of music that you develop in yourself the musical feeling. And if you only hear the music by radio or by gramophone records, then you are a spectator of music. You take the music from outside, at a distance, and so you receive the effect, but not of the real musical feeling. That is the point. I think the public today is a bad public, a public un-educated; most of the hearers know the music only by hearing, not by participating.

If they then know the music only by hearing, you are saying that it is something that is superficial.

Well, it may be that there are some of these hearers who will make the inner event of music. But not all. They can only remain as spectators.

Therefore, one really comes to the recording industry as such. Are you really pleased with the developments that have taken place in the recording, in the purveying of music, or do you think that there are quite a few ills that are attendant upon developing a large recording market?

No, I think it is very good, this recording. I was very much interested in recording. But I must say that it is extremely difficult. Perhaps other conductors are more clever or happier than I am in recording, because they remain cold and they can judge. I find it is always for me a terror. I know that what we are playing now is definitive. We remain on the record, you see, and I am afraid not to be exact, sufficiently exact.

In the public performance, in the concert, it is not so. We are quite free. What will happen will happen. We do our best, but we have no preoccupation with the absolute exactitude of each point, which is the case in recording. That is why I can say—and it is a confession—I am not sure that my records give the right idea of what I am able to do with some works. I am persuaded that I have given many performances of works I have recorded which were better than my recording; perhaps, in the recording, I was too absorbed by the sorrow of being exact.

You used the word definitive. Do you ever regard any performance as definitive?

No, no! We try to make the performance as perfect as possible. But after each occasion I think that next time it will be better!

I would like to ask you, Mr Ansermet, about some of the actual recording processes in a studio. Are you a believer in doing a work as a complete entity, or do you agree to splicing in fragments and doing things in short takes?

I must say, since we have the long-playing record we can make longer fragments and it is much better. Of course, we don't succeed always in making a full work, so we must make fragments. Or we can make them whole and take again a part of it, a few tags. But I can tell you, for instance, that our recording of *L'Après-Midi d'un Faune* was made at once. I told my orchestra, 'You are ready now—we are going till the end so that we have the unity.' We were sure of that unity.

But do you feel that in introducing these tags you destroy the unity?

Oh no, because when I make the tags I make them exactly as before, but it is better performed.

In discussing this business of splicing we are talking about a mechanical thing that is imposed upon music, and there is an increasing intrusion of the mechanical into our lives. Do you feel with the mechanical advances made in recording that they are all to the good?

Not always. Because in the first years when we were making stereo the microphones were placed before the orchestra and they took the whole orchestra at once. Now, they place several microphones in the orchestra and that may alter the balance established by the conductor. For instance, if I conduct I make the balance between my horns, trombones, strings and woodwinds.

Now if they take it with a microphone placed in the brass, they will give more value to the brass than I have given myself. That is a danger. I think in this progress, or so-called progress, of the technique is a danger. I told our technician, 'You are trying now to make a photo-

graph of the orchestra, because you place your microphones everywhere. But no, you have not to take a photograph, you have to take a
reproduction of the sound I produce myself with the whole orchestra.'
Sometimes the orchestra has too much of a concrete presence, a sonorous presence, than a musical presence.

At the beginning of our collaboration with Decca, our records had
very good success, and after two or three years I had the opportunity
of going to London to visit the Decca factory where the records are
made. One of the technicians in this factory asked me, 'Can you
explain to me why your records are so clean sounding?' I told him
perhaps the reason: 'You have before you a nice lady. She is of very
good appearance—nice clothes, and so on—but you don't know if,
under the clothes, the underwears are clean. I can tell you my effort is
to make clean the underwears!'

Geneva, September 1968

Otto Klemperer

PETER HEYWORTH: *Dr Klemperer, do you remember your very early years in Breslau?*

OTTO KLEMPERER: Oh yes, naturally.

How old were you when you left?

We left when I was four years old. From there my parents went to Hamburg and there I was until my sixteenth year. Then I went to study music.

That must have been a very big change, from Silesia to Hamburg, in atmosphere. Do you feel yourself to be more sympathetic to the Hanseatic atmosphere?

Oh yes, I feel myself absolutely as a Hamburger.

Not as a Silesian?

No, no. I have only one, but very strong, remembrance of Breslau. We went in the afternoon on a promenade and a very big, black dog came and sprang on my shoulders and I cried as a child, naturally, and then I had always a terrible fright of dogs, a fear, and always again in other forms I saw a black dog or black person; that is not good.

In Hamburg my first impressions from the train were the round *Litfassäulen*—the big pillars with the announcements of concerts and theatres and so on—and that was very fascinating for me; later they played a most important role in my life.

Because you returned there later as conductor, didn't you, at the Opera?

Yes. Yes. Later, much later.

What were your first musical experiences? When you look back, what are the things that immediately strike your mind?

At first—I think I was very young, six years old—I had piano lessons from my mother. She was a very good professional piano teacher and I was a very bad pupil. I always said, 'No, I want it so, and so.' And so I got a teacher, a very good man, very famous in Hamburg, and I learned with him every week. I studied with him the Inventions of Bach, the *Well-Tempered Clavier*, and I stayed with him up to Beethoven sonatas, chamber music, trios, and so on; he gave me lessons until my sixteenth year. And then I went to Frankfurt and Dr Hoch's Conservatorium, that was very famous in Germany.

Before I went, there came a friend of my mother, Mr Max Mayer, a pianist from Manchester, and he was to decide whether I had enough talent to be a musician. I played for him, I remember, a sonata of Philipp Emanuel Bach (not of Johann Sebastian) and a Beethoven sonata. Then he examined my ear and I said the right tones, and he asked me whether I had written something—composed—and I had. But I played for him a little piece, very childish, and he said, 'Now, that's not very important.' Then he said to my mother, 'I cannot tell you that your son will be a Hans Richter—I don't know—but in any case I'm sure he can become a good musician.'

From the very start, the intention when you went to the Conservatory was to be a conductor?

Everybody said, 'Be a musician,' and I said, 'All right.' But I thought later, when I was alone: I will become an actor. That was my strong wish. But it was never fulfilled.

But as a musician it was always conducting that attracted you—you never thought of being a professional pianist?

I tell you, at first I wanted very much to be a conductor. I saw other conductors, and then I played publicly. I was always so afraid that my hands became wet. My piano teacher was a very good man—James Kwast, a Dutchman—but he said, 'Always you play much better in the lessons than in public. You are not the same in public.' And he was right.

My first engagement as a real conductor was in Prague, but that was 1907. Before that I worked as a pianist—accompanist and pianist—and it was very important for me. We made the last big tour with a Dutch cello player, Jacques van Lier, and we went to different places and three times to Vienna.

And then in Vienna I went to Mahler. I played for him the Scherzo of his Second Symphony and he seemed to be very satisfied. I asked him to give me a recommendation. 'That is not necessary,' he said, 'A recommendation can be *gefälscht*—faked—therefore go to Rainer Simons [who was the Director of the Volksoper, not the Royal Opera House] and tell him I sent you, and it will be all right.' I did so, but it was not all right. He said, 'Thank you for your visit. Good morning.' I came back to Mahler and said, 'It's all in vain; it is absolutely necessary that I have a written recommendation from you.' And he took a little card of his, and wrote it, and I tell you, this recommendation, it opened for me every door.

The next day I went back to Berlin and there I made a photograph, about fifty copies of this recommendation, and sent it to twelve theatres in Germany to hope for a final engagement. But Mahler had said, 'It's always the first engagement which is so difficult; later on it comes by itself, but the first, naturally, you have difficulties.'

There was every year a meeting of an association for new music—I think Liszt was the founder—and in 1907 it was in Dresden. I thought: I will go to Dresden (I was a member of this society); perhaps something will happen. And I went to Dresden and was sitting in a restaurant alone, and on the other table there were two gentlemen and I heard what they talked about. One said, 'We need in Prague a young conductor.' I mean, don't you know, I was willing to stand up and say, 'Here he is!', but I didn't dare. So I asked a waiter who these two men were. One was Dr Richard Batka from Prague and the other Dr Marsop from Munich, musicologists. I went then to Dr Batka's hotel, and there the concierge told me he had departed that moment. So I went to the station and in the waiting room I found this Dr Batka and I gave him my card, and the card of Mahler, and he said, 'Yes, yes, you are the right man.' 'Here, this is crazy—how can you know that I am the right man?' 'Yes, I know it all right. You go to Marienbad; there is Angelo Neumann, the manager of the Prague Theatre. Tell him that I recommend you also, and then you will see what happens.' And I did so.

The whole night I travelled from Dresden to Marienbad. In the morning I went to Neumann and I took with me a big packet of compositions. I thought I must show him anyway. But he was not at all interested and he said only, 'Mahler, yes. Come to Prague and you will be the leader of the chorus and you will also conduct. What will you conduct?' I was so enthusiastic that a man offered me to conduct, I said, 'I'll do *Carmen*, and perhaps *Der Freischütz* and *Rigoletto*.' And he said, 'Bravo, all right, you do that.' Now the discussion seemed to be finished. But I said, 'But Mr Neumann, I must have from you a written document. I have made other wrong steps with other theatre directors.' And he gave me such a paper, like a contract. I was engaged for five years with a salary, not high, and I arrived the 15th August in Prague. And there the man in the office said, 'What's your name? What do you want?' I said, 'I am engaged here.' 'Where? Here? Mr Neumann has engaged you and has said nothing to us? I don't know.' So I took the letter from Neumann and then it was all right. And fourteen days later I conducted *Der Freischütz*.

That was the first opera you ever conducted?

No, no, not the first. I conducted in Berlin for fifty evenings *Orpheus in the Underworld* of Offenbach, because Max Reinhardt wanted me to do at first an Offenbach piece with his actors, not with singers. The conductor of this experiment was Oskar Fried—he was also the leader of the Stern'sche Gesangverein and I was his accompanist—and so he asked me whether I would help him in this thing. And I helped him. Two days after the beginning of the rehearsals there was trouble, terrible trouble. So in the third performance I conducted.

So that in a sense you started conducting by chance?

By chance, absolutely. It was a great thing for me that Max Reinhardt had said, 'All right, then we take Klemperer.' I mean that he trusted me that I could do it. And then began my career, if you will, in Prague, 1907.

You had already met Mahler earlier, hadn't you?

Yes, in Berlin, twice. At first, Oskar Fried conducted his Second Symphony. Mahler came to the rehearsals. I had to conduct the music behind the orchestra—trumpets and horns and so on. And I did it. And when I went to Mahler and said, 'Excuse me, but was that all right?', he said, 'No! It was terrible.' I said, 'What was terrible?' He said, 'It was too loud.' 'But', I said, 'it is written *sehr schmetternd*'—it is a word for 'very loud'—'In the score it is written very loud.' He said, 'But at a long distance. There it was much too close; we must go back.' So I said to the musicians, because it wasn't possible to go back, 'Play *piano*, only *piano*, the whole thing.' And they did it, and the performance was an enormous success. Mahler embraced Fried on the stage, and when he came into the artists' room he shook my hand and said, 'Very good.' I was proud.

Was this your first encounter with Mahler's music?

No, no. I studied theory with a man in Berlin, Mr Philipp Schar-wenka, a very good teacher. He said Mahler is a great composer. But I didn't know a work. And Nikisch gave the next week the first perform-ance of his Fifth Symphony, and I heard it. I was very disappointed. I could not find where the big force was.

What year was that?

Perhaps 1905 or 1906. Mahler at that time lived very far from the Philharmonic Orchestra and he asked, 'Where is Augsburgerstrasse?' I said, 'If you will allow, I will accompany you.' And I went with him to the elevator train—it was absolutely new, but he was not interested in these things. He said to me, 'You are composing?' I said no, I couldn't call my works compositions. 'Yes, yes,' he said, 'I know, I know, I see that you compose.' I was very proud.

Did he look at your compositions?

No, no, not at all, only at my face. And then he came in the same winter to Berlin and conducted himself his Third Symphony; and there I heard him rehearse for the first time. I saw how he conducted. It was very, very good. And also people like Pfitzner, who are not at all the friend of Mahler's music, I remember said, 'He is a colossal conductor.'

What was so remarkable about him as a conductor?

That's very difficult. I think at first one cannot learn it and one cannot teach it. That is important. Today, these conductor lessons— that is nonsense. I mean, the conducting where I give four so, and I give three so, I can tell you in three minutes; but that's all I can tell you. Not more.

But what made Mahler so remarkable as a conductor?

His tempi. One felt it could not be otherwise. That was it. And in a period when he was younger he is said to have had enormous movements, but I never heard it. I heard him a few years before his death and there he was very economical—not so economical as Richard Strauss, but very economical. Also in that year physicians told him he had a bad heart and he must be careful. Then he was very careful because he wanted to live for a long time. He was very chaste.

If we heard Mahler conducting today, would we feel his performances to be very romantic?

No. I tell you. I mean, the most famous conductor in the whole world was Toscanini, and he was a great man. I tell you Mahler was one hundred times better as a conductor. I mean, Toscanini, especially his performance of Beethoven, was sometimes very, very disputable. But Mahler, never. I heard him several times. There was for me only one thought: to give up this profession immediately if one cannot conduct like he did. Why conduct? It was enormous.

But your first great experience of Mahler's music was the Second Symphony in 1906; this is what started your enthusiasm for Mahler?

Yes, and when I knew the *Kindertotenlieder* and found the *Lieder eines fahrenden Gesellen*. And still today. I mean, I am not a stupid, enthusiastic boy: I don't like everything he wrote. But most of it. I conducted the Fourth Symphony, the Seventh just now—there are records—the Ninth Symphony, *Das Lied von der Erde*. The First I conducted only once in my life, in Cologne, but I don't like at all the last movement.

What about the Sixth?

I know. I know this is a very complicated work with an enormous last movement, a cosmos. But I have never conducted it.

Could I ask another question that has been on our minds? A number of great conductors have interpreted Mahler—Walter, Mengelberg and yourself—obviously with different emphasis on different parts of Mahler's musical personality. Can one then say there is such a thing as a tradition?

No, there is no tradition. But it is very characteristic that Mahler, who was so much for the tradition, said, 'Tradition is *Schlamperei*.'[1] You understand that, for his own works, there is no tradition.

No, though of course he didn't come to conduct Das Lied von der Erde *himself, did he?*

[1]Literally, 'slovenliness'.

No, not *Lied von der Erde*, nor the Ninth Symphony. Both works were first performed after his death.

The two greatest, do you think?

The Ninth Symphony I think is the greatest. Greater than, for my taste, the Eighth. But the Ninth Symphony, this is the climax for me.

You have said that you haven't conducted the Fifth and the Sixth for personal reasons. What do you mean by that?

I don't like to very much. I like in the Fifth the 'Marche Funèbre'—the beginning—I like that very much. Then the Scherzo is for me much too long, and not very interesting. And also the Adagietto, the little piece only for strings and harp, that's very nice; but it is near a salon piece. I mean, it is not enormous and the last movement again is much too long, and so I never conducted it.

The Sixth—that's another thing. I myself played, in the Sixth, celesta, as a student in Berlin; Oskar Fried conducted, and I think Mahler was present, yes. It's a great work and the last movement is really enormous, a tract of human life, life and death—a major chord followed by a minor chord; that is characteristic. And he conducted this in 1906 in Essen at the Internationales Musikfest.

What about Deryck Cooke's realization of the Tenth Symphony?

Scandal! I mean, at first, Mahler said to his wife, 'Burn the sketches of the Tenth Symphony when I am dead.' She did not. They were sketches. The only movement which is completed is the Adagio, and I conducted the Adagio. And then I heard—terrible moment!—that a man, whose name was Cooke, did this thing and I asked for the score and I saw the score. It's impossible.

Do you think there is not enough material there to make a version? Do you feel that the sketches are not a sufficient basis?

Not at all, because they are sketches, sometimes only a few notes on one line. And so, no. If Cooke were a second Mahler, then all right.

You made a piano reduction for two hands of the Second Symphony. What happened to that?

I don't know.

It's lost?

Lost. I took it to America and once I offered it to Schirmers—that is the music publishers in New York—but they didn't take it. They thought it was too difficult. I cannot tell you where it was lost—the many travels from America to Europe and Europe to America, later on in Australia. And so it's lost.

Is it true that when you were a very small boy you saw Mahler walking in the street?

Oh yes. You see, we lived in West Hamburg and there also Mahler lived. I went out and I saw beside me a very amusing man who could not go. . . .

He limped. . . .

Yes, yes. I knew—I don't know how—that it was Mahler, the conductor Mahler from the Theatre.

What physical impression did he make—very small?

Very small, yes. I mean, there are two sides which I saw in his nature. At first an enormous energy; he did not make concessions. He had his idea of life and death and so on. But on the other side he could be very *gemütlich*. I remember after the rehearsals for his Seventh Symphony in Prague, which were mostly in the afternoon, he came back to his hotel and we went with him. He told us about his experience in America and, for instance, we asked him what he liked most in America. And he said, 'I tell you, the greatest experience was I conducted the *Pastoral* of Beethoven.' Imagine, a man of fifty years with this reputation—no orchestra in Germany or in Austria gave him the opportunity, but New York did!

Was he not also conductor of the Vienna Philharmonic Orchestra?

Only two years. Because he had too many rehearsals and the Philharmonic Orchestra doesn't like that. And they took, instead of Mahler, Hellmesberger, who was a very, very, very small musician, a violinist. But in those two years in Vienna, for instance, he made many, many very strong retouchings of Beethoven symphonies. But I tell you, when he conducted these, with his personality, one didn't feel or hear retouches. He always said, 'These retouches I have made for me, not for somebody else; when I conduct it I can take the responsibility, but no other man.' But the touches were, I must say, very courageous. For instance, in the Ninth Symphony, there were not four horns but eight horns. I mean, strong things.

What about yourself? Do you retouch Beethoven at all?

I retouch.

What retouches do you make?

I mean, I retouch not so much as Mahler did.

Because when you did the Ninth Symphony in London first you made no retouches, did you?

No, there were none.

But do you now make them?

Then I changed. I tell you, for instance, when there is in the first violins a melody or melodic theme which I want very much to dominate, then I give the same notes to the second violins so that both violins play it; and then the part of the second violins I give to the violas. So everything is there, only in other terms. And one must do it sometimes in the Schumann symphonies, one must.

I heard a rehearsal of Mahler's Eighth Symphony at München—not the performance, unfortunately—but there was a rehearsal for the solo singers and the orchestra, and Mahler conducted. And he was never ready. He was not finished, I mean. And so in the Eighth Symphony during the rehearsals he said, 'No, take this for two clarinets, or this alone, or louder, or softer.' Then he turned and said, 'If, after my death, something doesn't sound, then change it. You have the right to change; not only the right, the duty to change it.' Because—this is very good words for all those people who think: never touch the notes—the composer himself may touch the notes. Some years before his death he said, verbally, 'The trouble is I cannot orchestrate.' No, really, he never was satisfied. He *could* orchestrate, but not enough. I mean, he was always wanting more: more clarity, more sound, more dynamics.

What about repeats in Beethoven?

One must repeat.

In all cases?

No. But in the Ninth one must.

What about the Fifth?

Yes, one must. I did it so, and so. I did it not always the same way. Now, for instance, I would repeat if I would conduct the Fifth Symphony.

In her Memories *Alma Mahler says that you and one or two other young musicians helped Mahler in copying his music. But I think in your own memoirs you say that Mahler never let anybody touch his music.*

It is true. He did not allow anybody to help him, because he trusted nobody and he wanted to make himself his retouches.

Why do you think there is such special interest in Mahler today? Why do you think he has become so significant for so many composers?

I must tell you I don't know, I don't know. It's a miracle that after a time of *Verachtung*[1] now is a time of enormous *Jubilate*.

Was he a man of great general intelligence?

Yes, very much. You know that mostly the orthodox Jews in Bohemia liked very much the German classics in the nineteenth century. Before that, no. Also my father, who was born in Prague in the Ghetto: his father was a religious teacher, and he wanted that his sons know Goethe and Eichendorff and so on, you understand? This is very important. And Mahler, without doubt he knew Spinoza; whether he knew Maimonides[2] I don't know.

You said, somewhere in your memoirs, that Mahler was an outsider in the religious sense. Do you think he was a man who was religious or a man who had a longing to be religious?

No, he was religious. He was absolutely religious, only he was not a member of a dogma. He was at first. He was a Jew. In Hamburg already he was baptized and he became a Catholic. That was absolutely necessary when there was a possibility to be the Director of the Vienna Hofoper. One had to be a Catholic, there is no doubt. But he never was it in the dogmatic sense.

I was interested that you said your father came from Prague. So really your own background is basically Bohemian-Jewish?

Yes.

---

[1] Being despised.
[2] Twelfth-century Jewish philosopher.

Austrian-Jewish, more than German?

Not at all German.

I never realized that.

I mean, my father was born in Prague and he was the son of a religious teacher. My mother came from a family called Rée; they were French—from Spain—French emigrants. I mean, I have no German blood.

But not even really a German background in that sense.

My father had a very good voice, but he was an amateur; and my mother, as I told you, was a very good pianist. My first musical impressions are songs of Schubert and music of Mozart and Beethoven and Schumann, a little Brahms, not more. But I remember, for instance, I heard the first performance of *Tod und Verklärung* of Strauss when I was about fifteen in Hamburg. It made a great impression.

It must have seemed extremely exciting.

Oh very. I was very much excited.

When did you first hear a Wagner opera?

In Frankfurt, when I was at the Conservatory, I heard *The Ring*. There was a very good tenor at that time in Frankfurt, Burgstaller.

So you heard Tod und Verklärung *before you heard Wagner?*

Yes, before, but I was more excited at *Tod und Verklärung* than about *The Ring*. It was very interesting.

When you were in New York in 1933 the orchestra you conducted was Toscanini's. What did you feel about his conducting?

Toscanini? He was absolutely a man who knew what he wanted and he was absolutely capable to execute what he wanted. I could not always agree with what he wanted, but I admired him very much. I mean, I went to his rehearsals and I went to different places in the empty hall—and how he could make this sound! I said, 'This is a miracle.'

A special sort of sound?

Yes. Absolutely.

Yes, but you also do this. You also have a very special sound.

Yes.

And I wonder how it happens that one man stands in front of an orchestra. . . .

I don't know. This is a very mysterious thing. Well, I can perhaps say a few words. I mean, very important for the conductor and for the orchestra is the upbeat—not the downbeat but the upbeat; it makes the orchestra more attentive. And there I learned from Toscanini in New York, a first-rate conductor.

I heard many, many concerts. I remember the first concert. I heard the Haydn Symphony in D Major, called the *Clock* Symphony—wonderful, wonderful. And at that time he conducted Respighi, for me a terrible piece, but his performance was amazing. *The Pines of Rome,* I think, is the title.

Did you ever feel his tempi were very fast in allegro *movements?*

Yes, much too fast.

And his Wagner?

Very good. Very good.

That's what Ernest Newman always said.

Oh, I heard *Die Meistersinger* in Milano conducted by him. Excellent, excellent.

Which other conductors of the generation older than yourself did you particularly admire? Nikisch?

Naturally Mahler. You see, Nikisch was a virtuoso. He was very elegant and a very good conductor. I think he was not such a good musician as conductor. As conductor he was absolutely first-rate. He conducted wonderfully the Schumann symphonies, wonderfully. He conducted also Mahler, but he did not like it. But both Nikisch and Mahler were together in Leipzig at the Staatstheater long before. They were rivals. And so Nikisch always said, 'I can only conduct if I feel this music in my heart.' But I think that was true.

He had a very romantic approach?

Yes, very, very romantic. He conducted also Wagner, very good, and **Richard Strauss.**

What about Strauss himself as a conductor?

There's only one Strauss. Mind you, he was wonderful. When he conducted he gave only very little movements. But he succeeded in every performance with the orchestra, especially Mozart.

Did Strauss seem to have a new approach to Mozart?

I think he had. For instance, *Così fan Tutte* was nearly unknown. I mean, yes, it was given always in terrible arrangements with other titles, and naturally in German, and he was the first who saw the enormous value in this music. He accompanied also recitatives himself on the cembalo. He played wonderfully.

One summer I visited Strauss; it was in the thirties or 1928. I was there and Strauss came for a few days in the same hotel, Waldhaus, and I had the occasion to make some promenades with him. And then he said to me, 'You see, I cannot conduct Beethoven. I always must see a picture.' I said, 'Picture?' 'A programme,' he said. 'For instance, you see, the second movement of the Fifth Symphony—that is a farewell of the lover.' I said, 'Farewell of the lover?' 'Oh yes, because afterwards, when the trumpets begin, you see: let us go to higher goals.' And that was enough!

But he conducted Beethoven well, none the less?

No. The Fifth Symphony was not good. But, all in all, he was a splendid conductor, naturally. You see there the difference between Nikisch and Strauss and Mahler: Strauss and Mahler were composers. That's a big difference. Nikisch was a conductor—a very good conductor—but he wrote not a note.

Boulez said exactly the same thing to me once. Criticizing some conductors, he said, 'They can't compose; they're not composers.' So I said, 'But Klemperer and Furtwängler are not composers.' He said, 'Ah, but they are; they do compose.' And his point was that all the best conductors can compose. You would agree with this?

Yes, absolutely.

Would you put Boulez himself very high as a conductor?

Yes, very high. He is without doubt the only man now—not only in Germany, I mean in the world—who is a real conductor. I mean a personality.

You say that you think Boulez is alone among his generation, but if one looks at that photograph that was taken when Toscanini came to Berlin in 1929 or 1930 there is yourself, Walter, Furtwängler, Kleiber and Toscanini. One may judge them differently, but none the less at that period there was a great generation of conductors. Do you think that now there is a decline in the general level of conducting?

Yes, a strong retrograde. I mean, the whole trouble of this young generation is that they forget the steps. One cannot start conducting with *Wozzeck* and last one plays a Haydn symphony. One must begin with Haydn, and conduct also Mozart and Beethoven and Schubert, and then one can go on. Don't you agree? I mean, this is the trouble. They all have no way and they have no goal to the high point; they want immediately to be there. This is very bad. I tell you frankly, if today they would ask me for the New Philharmonia Orchestra a permanent conductor, who always is in London, and I should take a name, I wouldn't know. I wouldn't know.

The mediocrities, they are the emperors today, the kings. Mediocrity in all places. Is it not a shame that the Grand Opéra de Paris has not Boulez there as first conductor?

What about Mengelberg, did you hear him?

Well, he was a very good trainer, wonderful. The Concertgebouw Orchestra is his creation. I mean, it was wonderful. I think as a conductor he was first-rate in things like the Fifth Symphony of Tchaikovsky.

Would you put Karajan in the same category?

No! Karajan is a very talented conductor and a very good conductor. I heard, for instance, a performance of *Falstaff* in Vienna with Italian singers, really excellent. But I heard, later on, the Ninth Symphony in Lucerne, also with the Vienna Orchestra. It was terrible. After the Scherzo I left the concert hall.

In what way did it not please you?

Too quick, much too quick. And in the Ninth Symphony, really, the metronomes are good for Beethoven.

And I heard him some months before in Amsterdam. He conducted the Bruckner Seventh, very good. But, you see, the entrance for the conductor is very far away in Amsterdam and the conductor has steps and steps and steps until he is on the ground. To see Karajan, how he comes back—that is a special theatre: with open arms and compliments to all sides, and again he has the open arms. This is comic, amusing. But he conducted very well. And I think it was not necessary for him to make this theatre. He is a good man, he can conduct, finish. Why he is so addicted to applause, I cannot understand. But he has a very nice wife, that I must say, a charming person, from Paris. He is just the conductor for nineteen hundred and sixty-nine.

Zurich, September 1969

Leopold Stokowski

GLENN GOULD writes: 'Stokowski is not the easiest person in the world to interview, not through any lack of co-operation on his part, but simply because, at his age, virtually all the questions that can be asked have been. Over the years his answers, to some extent, have developed a certain veneer of efficiency and despatch. Consequently, when undertaking this interview in December of 1969 in his New York apartment, I determined to head, if possible, for more original ground. At some risk to the conventional interview format, I opted to invert the order of my questions and open with the sort of query I would normally save until last. It was the type of hopelessly hypothetical question which it is virtually impossible to answer on the spot but which, none the less, given the right chemistry or the right slant of the sun between interviewer and interviewee, does occasionally elicit a genuinely insightful response.

'This question was preambled by a dissertation of my own so long, indeed, that I recall Stokowski nursing a teacup and observing me in that delightfully sly way of his as if to say, "Whose interview is this anyway?" I told him that I had often fantasized about the possibility of having at one's disposal the raw material with which to build, if one so chose, entirely new cultural patterns, and having set the mood with a lot of very low-key, parenthetic matter, I put my question.'

Maestro Stokowski, if, by some technological miracle, we could transport you to a planet on which a race of highly-developed beings had, to all appearances, achieved a state of peaceful coexistence, and if, having determined that their lives were lived without reference to the notion we call 'art', wherein they appeared to have achieved a state of civilization higher than our own . . . firstly, would you want them to know about the 'artistic' manifestations of our world; and, secondly, what type of cultural tradition would you endeavour to impose upon them?

LEOPOLD STOKOWSKI: Think of our solar system, its colossal size. I have the impression that there are many solar systems, that ours is a very big one, but that there are others which are much larger. And that their distance from other solid bodies floating in the atmosphere, this distance is enormous. I have also the impression that not only is there endless space and the endless mass of the solar systems that are in that space, but there is endless time and endless mental power, that there are great masses of mind of which ours, in this little Earth that we live on, is only a small part. We all live on this same planet. We breathe the same air and we are under the power of the light which the sun gives. No sunlight, no existence on this Earth. We are all under the same conditions and it is our privilege to make the best of those conditions, of the air we breathe, of the light we receive from the sun, that life-giving light.

At present all over the world is war, so much destruction and so little compared with that destruction that is creative. Many minds who are in what we call war, those minds might have enormous creative power. But they are killed, smashed by the destruction. If one studies history, one sees a series of wars. One sees clearly that nobody wins any of those wars. Everybody loses. They are madness. They are the lowest form of intelligence. The men who control things at the top, they have this low form of intelligence. They create these wars. It is time all humanity understood.

The artist, then, is living under the same conditions, making the best of those conditions, realizing that no matter how much effort he gives to improve his art, no matter how great an effort, there is no limit upwards, no limit. No matter how much a great artist improves his art, develops it, there is no limit to further improvement, further reaching upwards. Art is like the deep roots of the great oak tree, and out of those roots grow many branches, many kinds of art: the dance, architecture, painting, music, the art of words, the art that Shakespeare had. In a marvellous way he understood those things, our faults, our strengths, how we struggle to live. I travel in many countries and I notice that Shakespeare is translated into the language of that country, is performed in that country. His poetry is read and he is not merely the artist of one country, but the artist of the world. What a wonderful solution to life! The artist of the world.

Although I am interested in everything in the universe, what I really deeply understand is the symphonic world, because I have lived in it all my life. That is all I really understand. I think it is good, because it brings together many persons, many personalities. The great necessity in a symphonic orchestra is co-operation, that we work together. We call it by other names, but it really is co-operation. Personally I prefer the rehearsals to the concerts, because there is in a rehearsal the possibility to try again, to do better and better certain moments. What the world needs today is more co-operation, less destruction, less hatred.

First of all it is our privilege and our necessity to try to realize what was in the soul of the composer, and to make that alive again. This is very difficult. One must realize that our system of notation is extremely limited. It is primitive beyond all possibility. We write black marks on white paper, and we write that it is G natural or G sharp or G flat—the mere facts of frequency. But music is a communication much more subtle than mere facts. So the best a composer can do when within him he hears a great melody is to put it on paper. We call it music, but that is not music; that is only paper. It is black marks on paper. Some believe that one should merely mechanically reproduce the marks on the paper, but I do not believe in that. One must go much farther than that. We must defend the composer against the mechanical conception of life which is becoming more and more strong today.

So I think that there are two kinds of artist: those that have a system which they apply to every kind of art, and those who have no system but create a different kind of system for each kind of art. If I had to perform the music of, say, Mozart or Shostakovich or Debussy, they all have their own world, their own kind of expression, and I am trying to understand their style and to use the methods—particularly the methods of phrasing—which are applicable to that style. I have noticed other conductors who have a system which they apply to any kind of style and the results are mechanical. They may be clear, definite, strong, but they are mechanical. They do not have that impulsive quality that is in the nature of art and of human life. Spontaneity is the reaction to conditions of life and that reaction should be extremely flexible.

I think that Ives had that freedom. Ives was an inspired amateur of music, like Borodin. Borodin was a chemist, and the fact that they were amateur gave them perhaps more freedom to start with than a young musician who is taught what is good and what is not good. Perhaps later that artist has to throw off the burden of what is good and what is bad and face the actual facts of his art. When we began studying

Ives's great Fourth Symphony, we found so many contradictions within. His music is full of contradictions within itself and yet that is so true to life. Some composers have no contradictions. Everything is according to their system, according to what they learnt in the conservatoire where they studied as a young child. We must give our education of music, of philosophy and of everything connected with human life, subtlety. We must give it elasticity, so we can bring into our conception of culture all the possibilities of life which are often very contradictory.

I knew Schoenberg; we were friends. Before he created his system, he composed the *Gurrelieder*—extraordinary music, wonderful, wonderful music, too seldom performed. It is on such a vast scale, it is difficult to perform it. It requires, for example, three separate choruses of men's voices. It is hard to find in any place three good choruses of men's voices. So it is seldom performed. But there came a time when Schoenberg began to develop his new system, quite different from *Gurrelieder*, and for the rest of his life he lived according to that system. When he had finished a new composition, he always sent it to me and we performed it first. He came and listened to the rehearsals and the performances, and changed many things, because his system was not rigid. It seems to be rigid, but it isn't. It was flexible, and he changed many things before they were later printed. It can all be expressed in one word. That one word is freedom. Freedom to think, to read, to write, to speak and to live, provided one does not take away freedom from other people. There are countries where one is free to think and speak and write as one wishes. There are other countries where that is not permitted. In a country where there is freedom the composer can put whatever marks he likes on paper. The performer can either perform it or not, as he wishes, because he is free. The listener can listen with an open mind, or listen already prejudiced against it. That is freedom; and those who indulge in such prejudice are their own enemies.

Shostakovich lives in an atmosphere where the arts are greatly appreciated. They have given Shostakovich every possibility to live quietly. But it has been difficult for him in other ways, because he is extremely original. To understand originality the understanding person has to have originality himself, and as this is a rare matter of the mind, Shostakovich has suffered, like every original person in the realm of science or philosophy. They all have suffered the difficulty that they are not understood by persons who are less original than they are. That is the price the human mind pays for being original, for being creative, for producing something which is quite different from everything that has been known from that country beforehand.

Music is never really drawn together tightly into a knot of one country, but is always international in spirit. I believe it will be from now on even more so. Because of communication, we shall have a music which expresses the emotions and dreams of men and women of every country. We can at the same time guard our national spirit. I notice this very much in Rumania. I go sometimes to Rumania to conduct and I am so delighted with the way they cultivate their folk music, their folk dances, and while this spirit lasts they will never lose their folklore. That country, Rumania, is remarkable for that. But all countries have their folklore. The United States is rich in folk music of the mountains, of the far West. I hope we shall guard that spirit which made it remarkable as melody and harmony and rhythm. The Americans today come from every land in the world, probably, and they gradually combine into one more or less clear conception of life. But there is very much differentiation within that conception, and it is a wonderful thing that in this vast land of North and Central America we have the cultures of all the other lands on this small Earth on which we live. And they are gradually combining and forming, possibly, an entirely new conception of life. That may take many centuries, but it may be a larger and broader and deeper conception of life.

It is remarkable that one can stay in the home and hear music from all over the world, hear music from a great distance and perhaps the actual sounds of that music made thirty or forty years ago. I remember —I think it was in the year 1917—that a recording company asked me to make records and I said, 'May I listen to some of your records?' and they permitted me to do that. They were so terrible, I said, 'No, I cannot distort music. Sorry, but no, I will not do it.' Then a little after that I realized how stupid I had been to refuse. I should try to make the records and, if they were bad, try to discover why they were bad, and do something about improving the quality. I thought to myself, 'You're a fool. You shouldn't have said no.' So I then said to them, 'Please forgive me, but may I try?' We did try and the records were not good. We had to put all the players into a huge wooden horn which carried the vibrations to the cutting needle. We could not use double basses because they did not sound under those conditions. Instead of double basses we had a tuba, just one tuba, to play that part. The results were, of course, horrible. But there came a day later on when fortunately we could record electronically.

In the meantime, I thought I must try to understand how it could be done electronically, so I asked the Bell Laboratory, 'Could I come to you and study electricity as regards recording music?' They permitted it and soon after that they said, 'We would like to create a laboratory underneath the stage of the Academy of Music in Philadelphia.' At that time I was the conductor of the Philadelphia Orchestra. Bell made a laboratory underneath the stage from which they listened to all our rehearsals and all our concerts and used that as material for the betterment of recording techniques. So gradually recording became better. It is better today, but I think it still could be much better.

In Holland, about twenty years ago, I was conducting the Concertgebouw Orchestra and the Philips Research Laboratory, one of the finest in the world and very open-minded to new ideas, said to me, 'Are you willing that we listen to all your rehearsals and your concerts and use them for a new idea we have?' And I said, 'May I know what is the new idea?' And they told me it was to listen from four corners of a room, so there would not be definite direction; we would sit in the middle of the room, there would be loudspeakers in the four corners and they would have a low intensity which would blend in the middle of the room. That we did a long time ago and now I am hoping it will be done all over the world for everybody.

I am very impressed by the fact that stereophonic recordings today are sometimes not truly stereophonic. They are pretending to be. The same signal is coming from the right channel as from the left channel, whereas half of the orchestra which is producing the tones on the left side should sound from the left loudspeaker and the other half from the right loudspeaker. That is how it should be, but sometimes it is not. As the vibrations come to the listener and to his ears, these tones are blended into one composite as it is in the concert hall.

But, of course, the concert hall is something we have known from our ancestors. Our grandfathers always heard the music from the stage, but I believe the time will come when we shall make records in the open air, where every instrument has its particular pick-up and is amplified to the right extent. All those sounds are then brought together into one composite, with the right intensity of amplification of each instrument at each moment, because sometimes the woodwind should be louder than the strings, or the brasses should be louder than everybody, or a certain percussion instrument should be louder than any other instrument. Or it could be done in a large enclosed space. But the point is that I should like to have a hundred results from each individual instrument and give them their due intensity or volume of sound according to that moment of the music. So this is all a question of balance, and by this means we could create such a perfect balance.

I find that every day come new possibilities and new ideas and they must not be ignored, they must be examined. For example, there are many kinds of sounds—don't be shocked at what I'm going to say, but I like the sound of street noises: taxi cabs are blowing their horns and all kinds of sounds are going on. They have a rhythm, they have a blending of life in the streets, and it is a kind of music. Some people would say that it is just a horrible noise, and they have a right to their opinion too. To their ears it *is* a horrible noise. To my ears it is interesting, because it is life. Those who think it is nonsense will either not listen at all or they will listen with prejudice, and prejudice is a very dangerous disease. The others will listen and perhaps will receive that mysterious message which is in all music, which words cannot express. Shakespeare used the word for dramatic reasons, but he also used the word for poetic reasons. He selected language which sounds to me like music. The words and the rhythms of the words are just like music to my ears.

It is quite possible that the so-called cave man had such ideas too, on his level, in his way, according to his ideas of the best life of that time. There have always been persons on this earth who love beauty and order. It is so important to know what we really do know, definitely, and to realize the immense mass of possibilities there are to life that we do not know. There may be corresponding forms of life on other planets. It is difficult to know what they are feeling and what they are thinking. Their life might be quite different from our human life or our animal life. Also there would be the question of language, the question of how we communicate. So it would be very difficult. Yet I would think it a great privilege if I could know their ideas of the best form of existence, their ideas about the creative life, their ideas of what is orderly and what is beautiful. That would be the first step, I think, to try and understand their life, to find out what they think and feel and dislike. If I did have that possibility, I would do my best to give a clear impression of what other form of life there might be on that planet, of what I think is beautiful and orderly, what I think is creative and what I think is destructive. It would be possible, I hope, to let them see what is happening on this Earth—so much destruction, so little that is creative.

But think of our solar system, its colossal size, its possibility.

New York, December 1969